T0311447

Cambridge Elements

Elements in Global Development Studies
edited by
Peter Ho
Zhejiang University
Servaas Storm
Delft University of Technology

DISPLACEMENT IN WAR-TORN UKRAINE

State, Displacement and Belonging

Viktoriya Sereda
National Academy of Sciences of Ukraine

CAMBRIDGE
UNIVERSITY PRESS

Shaftesbury Road, Cambridge CB2 8EA, United Kingdom

One Liberty Plaza, 20th Floor, New York, NY 10006, USA

477 Williamstown Road, Port Melbourne, VIC 3207, Australia

314–321, 3rd Floor, Plot 3, Splendor Forum, Jasola District Centre,
New Delhi – 110025, India

103 Penang Road, #05–06/07, Visioncrest Commercial, Singapore 238467

Cambridge University Press is part of Cambridge University Press & Assessment,
a department of the University of Cambridge.

We share the University's mission to contribute to society through the pursuit of
education, learning and research at the highest international levels of excellence.

www.cambridge.org
Information on this title: www.cambridge.org/9781009314497

DOI: 10.1017/9781009314473

First published 2023

A catalogue record for this publication is available from the British Library.

ISBN 978-1-009-31449-7 Paperback
ISSN 2634-0313 (online)
ISSN 2634-0305 (print)

Displacement in War-Torn Ukraine

State, Displacement and Belonging

Elements in Global Development Studies

DOI: 10.1017/9781009314473
First published online: June 2023

Viktoriya Sereda
National Academy of Sciences of Ukraine
Author for correspondence: Viktoriya Sereda, sereda.vik@gmail.com

Abstract: This Element offers a multi-scalar perspective on the transformational effects of war and dislocation on people's sense of belonging. It begins with an examination of the brief historical and socio-demographic profiles of Crimea and the Donbas, stages of the Russian-Ukrainian conflict, main explanatory frameworks as presented in the scholarly literature and policy reports, with a critical re-evaluation of identity-based explanations, and the directions of conflict-driven displacement flows. It examines state failures and the role of internal displacement governance in shaping new lines of social inclusion or exclusion through the production of multiple physical, symbolic, and bureaucratic borders. It discusses Ukraine's civil society response to internally displaced person dislocation and IDPs' engagement through various formal and non-formal networks. The final section explores the multidimensional and complex (dis)connections that IDPs experience with regard to their imagined past, their new places of residence, and the social groups perceived as important in their hierarchies of belonging.

The Element also has a video abstract: www.cambridge.org/sereda

Keywords: conflict-related migration governance, war and belonging, civil society and informal self-aid networks, Ukrainian IDPs and refugees, Donbas and Crimea, war in Ukraine

ISBNs: 9781009314497 (PB), 9781009314473 (OC)
ISSNs: 2634-0313 (online), 2634-0305 (print)

Contents

1 Introduction

This Element was almost completed before the entire world was stunned by Russia's massive military aggression against Ukraine in February 2022 and was intended to explore how war and intensive displacement from two regions – the Donbas and Crimea – (re)shaped narratives of belonging for the internally displaced people (IDPs) and the local communities in Ukraine receiving them. The Element initially set out to question the role of the state, and the local communities in these processes. How might attempts by national states to control the movement of IDPs – as well as their policies aimed at assisting them – affect existing social hierarchies of belonging and create lines of inclusion and exclusion through the production of multiple physical, symbolic, and bureaucratic borders. This leads to the discussion of civil society's response to Ukrainian states failures and how IDPs' engagement in various formal and non-formal self-aid networks help them to rearticulate their sense of belonging.

Many issues discussed in the study became even more pertinent after 2022, such as the new roles devolved on the state and civil society in assisting the IDPs and refugees, or the increasing weaponisation of refugee policies in the region. Many trends described in the Element help us to understand better the specifics of new displacement crises (both internal and cross-border). They demonstrate the undercurrent of transformative change occurring inside Ukrainian society before and after the Russian invasion, which made such strong resilience and support for the displaced possible. The Element also explains why the military conflict over the Donbas had been mistakenly portrayed as stemming from ethno-linguistic issues. Recently these arguments were repeated by Putin as justification for Russia's aggression against Ukraine. I believe that the particular significance of my research lies in pointing out several trends that have become even more salient after Russia's attack on Ukraine.

Firstly, the increasingly dangerous trends of the weaponisation of refugees (e.g., Russia's use of purposefully created movement of refugees in order to augment their regional influence or achieve certain political goals) and the intentional creation of humanitarian crises in besieged cities as a war tactic threatens to become an ever-growing challenge in the region as well as for the governance of global migration and conflict resolution.

Second is the 'invisibility' of Ukrainian IDPs in European migration research, as it has mostly considered migration as a cross-border phenomenon, and in so doing overlooked the phenomenon of internally displaced persons, a situation that is relevant in numerous societies. Traditionally, migration and the IDP phenomenon have been associated with the Global South, not with Eastern Europe. Since 2014, discussions about the crisis in Ukraine have repeatedly come to the fore, particularly with regard to peacekeeping and foreign policy agendas. By 2016, Ukraine had the largest number of IDPs in Europe and the fifth largest in the world, yet European media did not consider Ukraine in their internal debates about the 'migrant threat' in their respective countries. After the onset of Russian aggression, the media have mostly focused on refugees fleeing the country, but the critical situation and negative effects of that conflict on internal displacement within the country (currently the estimated ratio of those who crossed the border to the internally displaced is one in four) has received little attention, similar to 2014. Ukrainian society is also experiencing a double displacement as those were displaced after 2014 are now fleeing again.

However, what has radically changed after 2022 is the admission policies for Ukrainian refugees. After 2014 neighbouring European Union (EU) countries tried to manipulate the situation, claiming that they had accepted close to a million refugees from Ukraine (in reality they were documented and undocumented labour migrants who never applied for refugee status) in order to avoid accepting Syrian refugees. By 2021, Ukraine accounted for the largest number of IDPs in Europe, but this wave of displacement was mostly contained within the country. Ukrainian refugees had difficulties crossing the western (Schengen zone) border, and only 2 per cent of asylum-seeking applications were granted refugee status. With Russia's subsequent attempts to pressure the USA and its European allies into concessions on 'security guarantees' by amassing over 100,000 troops near the Ukrainian border, experts have been discussing the consequences of aiding Ukraine in the event of a Russian invasion; the threat of a large wave of Ukrainian refugees has been at the centre of such discussions.[1] However, nobody predicted the real scale of the refugee crisis, which turned out to be the biggest European population displacement since the end of the Second World War. This time the EU and many other countries demonstrated their highest level of support by adopting fast and efficient admission policies.

Finally, I want to stress that the current global migration governance approach presupposes that the primary responsibility for offering humanitarian aid and preserving the rights of IDPs falls on their own states, and in the case of refugees, on the receiving state and international organisations. My study illustrates that in their efforts state and over-bureaucratised international organisations may fall far behind the new forms found in civil society. Since 2014, the conflict-induced displacement in Ukraine stimulated an unprecedented wave of

---

[1] Krastev, I. and Leonard, M. (2022). The crisis of European security: What Europeans think about the war in Ukraine. *ECFR*, 432, available at: https://ecfr.eu/wp-content/uploads/2022/02/the-crisis-of-european-security-what-europeans-think-about-the-war-in-ukraine.pdf, accessed 9 February 2022.

social mobilisation, the emergence of a new type of social activism and a new quality of civil society in Ukraine. These processes require special attention as they prepared Ukrainian society for unprecedented resistance and self-aid networking after the full-scale Russian invasion. Now, very similar processes are happening in the countries neighbouring Ukraine that are receiving refugees.

This study draws attention to issues that are relevant for both policymakers and academics interested in conflict-related migration governance. This Element offers a multi-scalar perspective on the transformational effects of war and dislocation on people's sense of belonging. The first section begins with an examination of the main causes of the Russian-Ukrainian conflict as presented in the scholarly literature and policy reports, with a critical re-evaluation of identity-based explanations.

The second section examines state failures and the role of internal-displacement governance in shaping new lines of social inclusion or exclusion through the production of multiple internal, physical, symbolic, and bureaucratic borders and their impact on the IDPs' sense of belonging. Section 2 further discusses the civil society's response to IDP dislocation and its engagement through various formal and non-formal networks. It discusses the specifics of civil society mobilisation – a wide variety of forms of engagement and self-aid initiatives. The section on the response of the civil societies helps us to understand how new challenges in the experience of displacement can be addressed by a civil society, and how civil societies can help displaced people to overcome the deficiencies of state support and resources in order to build a new sense of belonging through participation. In the final section, I explore the multidimensional and complex connections and disconnections that IDPs experience with regard to their imagined past or mnemonic practices, their new places of residence and the social groups that they perceive as important in their hierarchies of belonging.

A conflict-sensitive approach calls for a deeper understanding of the local context, the existing power dynamics and the attribution of causes. In what follows, I provide a brief historical overview of the regionally specific and socio-demographic profiles of Crimea and the Donbas. I also describe the context and the key stages of the Russo-Ukrainian conflict over the Donbas and Crimea, and the directional flow of internal displacement within the country and across borders. I further provide an overview of resettlement patterns and the structural specifics of Ukrainian IDPs, who do not constitute a socially, politically, religiously, or ethnically homogeneous group.

Within the Element I will engage in the analysis of various forms of 'borders and orders' (such as the 'experts' discourse on the conflict's character, national legal norms, and bureaucratic regulations concerning government responses to migration and the displaced) to expose anxieties and concerns about the borders, identities, and hierarchies of belonging in the affected countries. I use a multi-scalar perspective on the transformational effects of war and dislocation on people's sense of belonging.

This monograph analyses the inter-relation between the process of migration and the re-articulation of the sense of belonging by both resettled groups and receiving communities and the role of multiple physical, symbolic, and legal/ bureaucratic borders within the society ('borders and orders') in this process. I also look at the civil society as an important factor in building a stronger sense of belonging as well as new lines of inclusion. This study borrows conceptual tools from the 'everyday nationalism' approach with its orientation towards the study of practices, symbolic systems, and state institutional arrangements that account for the everyday (re)production of frameworks of belonging (Skey, 2011).

The concept of belonging reveals the relationship between the self and the collective, 'official', and 'unofficial' spheres (one of which is civil society) at the level of everyday experiences (Yuval-Davis 2011; May 2013). I believe that the term 'belonging' better conveys the relationship of the individual with society, as it includes in the analysis, not only the interaction with groups or individuals but also the interaction with spaces and cultures, and understands people as active participants in society (Griffith, 1995; Probyn, 1996; May, 2011). Guibernau (2013) stresses the relational character of belonging and identifies two types of belonging – belonging as a choice or as imposed by others (exclusion) – when the receiving community sets some symbolic or physical borders, that is, where state regulation over migration plays a crucial role. Thus, I believe that 'belonging' is a category that allows me to address both the institutional and the community or individual level of migration governance, particularly the integration of the migrants, refugees or IDPs, and to observe it as a two-way process.

1.1 Brief Historical and Socio-Demographic Profiles

1.1.1 Crimea

For over six centuries, the Crimean Peninsula was under the jurisdiction of Tatar Khanate, which from the late fifteenth century was integrated into the Ottoman Empire. At that time, its population was diverse with a predominance of Crimean Tatars. In 1783, during the Russo–Turkish wars, the Khanate was taken over by the Russian Empire. As a result of the imperial colonisation policy, Crimean Tatars left the peninsula en masse, and new settlers were given their land, especially after Russia's defeat in the Crimean War (1853–56). By 1864, the Crimean Tartars' population on the peninsula dropped to 50.3 per cent and by the end of the century (1897 census) to 35.6 per cent. The largest groups of new settlers consisted of Russians at 33.1 per cent, Ukrainians at 11.8 per cent, and Germans at 5.8 per cent, although, the peninsula – especially the harbour cities – hosted many different ethnic groups including Armenians, Bulgarians, Greeks, Gagauzs, Jews, Karaites, and Krymchaks (Bekirova et al., 2020).

After the turbulent years of the collapse of the Russian Empire, which was followed by the Bolsheviks' seizure of power and a civil war, Crimea became dominated by the new Soviet regime. Until 1945, it was an autonomous republic within Soviet Russia. In 1954, it was transferred to Soviet Ukraine.

According to the 1939 census, the Russian population on the peninsula had already reached 50 per cent; meanwhile, the population of Crimean Tatars had dropped to 19 per cent, and yet, the Soviet government still considered them to be a threat. In 1944, by Stalin's decree, all Crimean Tatars, including over 40,000 Bulgarians, Armenians, Greeks, Turks, and Roma were deported from the Peninsula. Deportation had a devastating impact on the demographic making up Crimea leading to the total loss of its indigenous population (leaving 0.0 per cent Crimean Tatars and other deported groups) and the destruction of its unique multi-ethnic and multicultural character. After the Second World War, Crimea was turned into one of the Soviet Union's key military outposts (with Kerch and Sevastopol becoming a city-military base practically closed to the public) along with recreational and retirement areas for the Soviet elite and resorts for common Soviet citizens. The 1959 census showed that the absolute majority of the peninsula now consisted only of Russians (71 per cent) and Ukrainians (22 per cent).

The repatriation of the deported ethnic groups began after the implementation of Perestroika in 1989. Those who returned were neither entitled to the restitution of their pre-deportation property, nor could they buy it officially due to the absence of private property rights for real estate and land in the Union of Soviet Socialist Republics (USSR). The Crimean Tatars' situation depended on the willingness of local authorities to grant them land rights or local registration ('propyska'). For years, this was the source of many discriminatory practices, mutual hostility, and even pogroms in the returnees' temporary settlements.

Post-1991

In 1991, with the collapse of the Soviet Union and the proclamation of Ukraine's independence, the local Crimean pro-Russian authorities held a referendum. The outcome of the referendum was a change in the region's status to an autonomous republic, shifting the distribution of power to the governments of Kyiv and Crimea. As a result, local authorities had even more power over the arriving returnees. In 1998, the Crimean Tatars proposed an amendment to the new Autonomous Republic's constitution that would guarantee quotas for the political representation of minorities. However, this proposal was rejected. According to the last Ukrainian census (2001), ethnic Russians made up 58.5 per cent of the Peninsula's population, Ukrainians made up 24.4 per cent, and Crimean Tatars made up 12.1 per cent (by 2013, they had reached 13.4 per cent) (Derzhavnyi Komitet Statystyky Ukrainy, 2001).

In spite of such historical tensions, prior to the 2014 crisis, Crimea was considered 'a success story of post-Soviet conflict prevention' (Sasse, 2007). As time passed, experts stated that the number of confrontations had decreased, and that both groups were gradually learning to coexist. In 2010, Gwendolyn Sasse (2010, p. 103) described the situation in the peninsula in the following terms: 'The separatist movement in Crimea in the early 1990s was defused by political means, national and regional elites reached a step-by-step accommodation and marginalised the more militant nationalist elements in both Kyiv and Crimea while breaking the link between Crimea's Russian nationalists and Moscow. It helped that Crimea's multiethnicity undermined clear-cut ethnopolitical mobilisation'. A survey of the local population conducted a year later supports this argument by demonstrating that a sense of regional identity ('living in Crimea') was the most salient and territorial factor of identity among Crimeans of all ethnic backgrounds (Charron, 2016).

1.1.2 Donbas

The Donbas region has a different story. It is a relatively young region, whose formation is linked to accelerated industrialisation and the Russian Empire's need for inexpensive fossil fuels. Since the 1870s – after the discovery large coal reserves – mining and metallurgy industries have developed to include a strong presence of international (mostly European) capital, which in turn, has attracted workers from the neighbouring regions of Russia and Ukraine. By the end of the Russian Empire, the Donbas was the most rapidly industrialised region, but suffered from significant social tension later becoming an important base for the Bolshevik party. In his study of the Donbas, Hiroaki Kuromiya shows that both the imperial government and the Soviet officials found it difficult to control the local labour force – which was portrayed as intractable and prone to outbursts of violence in the form of riots, strikes, or pogroms. The new Bolshevik regime tried to use the Donbas as an outpost against the

Ukrainian National Republic[2] and organised their so-called 'Donetsk-Kryvyi Rih Soviet Republic'. In 1919, the Donbas became a part of Soviet Ukraine. In 1938, as a result of several Soviet administrative reforms, two administrative regions were formed: Stalin (today Donetsk) and Voroshylovohrad (today Luhansk) *oblast.*

After the Second World War, the Donbas not only became an industrial borderland for the Soviet authorities, but it also became an important 'showcase' region, where the new type of socialist industrial society was to be built. Its cities were often called 'garden-cities' in order to compensate for the previous rapid urbanisation. By means of the Soviet planned economy, the region was strongly tied to industries located in Russia and other Soviet republics, which underlines its importance for the Soviet Union.

The development of the Donbas was accompanied by processes of intensive urbanisation, migration, and the formation of a particular urban way of life (often built around one town-forming enterprise or mine that not only provided jobs but also social services). It attracted settlers from many different regions (limited to Soviet geography) and gradually assimilated them into Russian culture, officially designated as the high culture of the Soviet Union (Yekelchyk, 2016). These processes contributed to the formation of an important regional myth about the Donbas, that is, that it was the most important economic region in the entire country (the USSR). This encouraged feelings of great pride among the inhabitants of the Donbas for their professional and regional/urban status (Kuromiya, 1998; Osipian, 2015).

From about the 1960s onwards, this myth gradually lost touch with reality when the USSR decided to prioritise oil and gas production over coal, and to reorient its industry and investments towards new sources of energy (including nuclear). These changes had a significant impact on the life of the region. As with other industrial European regions, when coal mining gradually became economically uncompetitive, the Donbas began to experience increasing socioeconomic hardship. However, the myth of the Donbas' economic strength was still relentlessly exploited in order to cover up such problems.

Statistically, the Donbas had the largest concentration of ethnic Russians, after Crimea, in Soviet Ukraine. According to the 1926 census, 64 per cent of the Donbas population were identified as ethnic Ukrainians while 26 per cent were Russian. The Russian population dominated the big cities, which were surrounded by the Ukrainian-speaking countryside. By 1989 (the final Soviet census), the percentage of ethnic Russians had increased to 44 per cent and the

---

[2] The Ukrainian National Republic was the short-lived Ukrainian state that emerged after the collapse of the Russian Empire, 1917–20.

Ukrainian population had decreased to 51–52 per cent. After the collapse of the Soviet Union, this trend reversed. In the most recent census, made in 2001, ethnic Russians represented 38 per cent of the Donbas population and Ukrainians 57–58 per cent (Derzhavnyi Komitet Statystyky Ukrainy, 2001; Maliarchuk, 2011). However, these statistics might be misleading[3] and tell us very little about the national self-identification processes happening in the region.

Post-1991

When Ukraine became independent in 1991, its economy – especially the Soviet industrial regions – suffered a devastating economic decline and experienced an extremely slow and painful transition to the new market economy. According to Vlad Mykhnenko (2011), 'Ukraine's post-Soviet development was characterised by the deepest and longest economic depression experienced by any of the post-communist transition economies not affected by war, resulting in the loss of 60 per cent of the gross domestic product (GDP) between 1990 and 1999'. These transformations were especially painful for the Donbas region and its population, and they created perfect conditions for the resurrection of 'the great Donbas' myth and for Soviet (specifically Soviet-Ukrainian) nostalgia, which was used by the local elite to mobilise their political supporters. As a result of this mobilisation in the Donbas region, a party was established in the late 1990s called the 'Party of Regions', which, after the Orange Revolution of 2004, grew to be the biggest party in the Ukrainian parliament.

The party was positioned as defending the region's economic interests and the rights of the Russian-speaking population; it further argued for closer cooperation with Russia and stood as the opponents of the pro-democratic and pro-EU parties. Viktor Yanukovych was the Party's head when, in 2010, he became the President of Ukraine. Significantly, prior to 2014, neither the Donbas nor Crimea had a strong pro-Russian party in their political landscape. When the Euromaidan protests took place across Ukraine, these two regions were rather on the margins; there were sporadic pro-Euromaidan protests while sentiment against the Euromaidan movement built gradually.

---

[3] In the census questionnaire, the question that was officially presented as 'nationality' was formulated in line with the Soviet-ascribed approach to nationality, asking 'what is your ethnic origin?'

1.2 Stages of the Russo-Ukrainian Conflict over the Donbas and Crimea and the Directions of Conflict-Driven Displacement Flows

1.2.1 Euromaidan

In November 2013, after the rapid change in Ukraine's geopolitical course that was brought about by Viktor Yanukovych's government, street protests evolved into a massive political upheaval, known as 'Euromaidan' or the 'Revolution of Dignity'. Throughout the winter of 2013–2014, protesters demonstrated an unprecedented level of civil solidarity and readiness to sacrifice their time, resources and even their lives in the name of European integration and rule of law, and were in opposition to authoritarian politicians and corruption. After 16 January 2014, when the government introduced a series of repressive laws severely restricting civil society and the right to protest, clashes between the protestors and the riot police escalated. They culminated on 20 and 21 February, when over a hundred people – mostly civilian protesters, later called the Heavenly Hundred heroes, and seventeen police officers – were killed in clashes. On 21 February, an agreement was signed between the president and the leaders of the parliamentary opposition which called for early elections and the formation of an interim unity government. However, the next day, President Yanukovych fled the country. Parliament voted to oust him and held new elections in May.

1.2.2 The Annexation of Crimea

Immediately after Yanukovych's escape, pro-Russian demonstrations escalated in Crimea and covert Russian troops bearing no insignia began to mount up. Later that month, they took over the strategic sites across Crimea and supported the installation of the pro-Russian government in the peninsula. On 16 March 2014, the so-called 'Crimean status referendum' was conducted. The international community did not recognise the referendum as legitimate. Russia used the referendum's results as a formal pretext which allowed them to annex the peninsula and incorporate Crimea as a federal part of Russia on 18 March 2014. This launched the first wave of displacement.

According to differing estimates (Smal, 2016), between 20,000 and 50,000 people left the Crimean Peninsula while some 2.4 million inhabitants found themselves behind the new dividing line. Since Russia annexed Crimea without open military conflict, most chose to leave not because of violence, but for fear of Russian state persecution of Crimean Tatars (especially the more observant Muslims) and those with pro-Ukrainian views. There were other reasons as well: emotional attachments to the Ukrainian state, the unwillingness to live on unrecognised territory or in the Russian state, and economic interests. The Crimean Tatars' situation differed from that of other IDPs, who could claim that by moving to Ukraine they had returned to their land of origin or their homeland. Because Crimean Tatars are the indigenous population of Crimea, they had left their homeland, which they had just recently reacquired, once again.

Crimean Tatar IDPs formed three large communities. Those who wanted to settle close to Crimea did so in the neighbouring region of Kherson. Those who wanted to be close to the central government and be able to voice their needs went to Kyiv. Finally, the most religious Muslims, for whom religiosity was the most important marker for belonging, went to Lviv, where people observe the most religiosity in the country albeit that the absolute majority were Christian.[4]

1.2.3 Beginning of the Conflict over the Donbas

From the end of February into March 2014, demonstrations by pro-Russian and anti-government groups took place in major cities across the eastern and southern regions of Ukraine. In March, there were several attempts to storm local administrative buildings (mostly in the Donbas) that were defeated by government law enforcement units who recaptured the buildings. In April 2014, the situation gradually escalated in the Donbas. The military conflict started with the military seizure of Slaviansk, commanded by Russian citizen Igor Girkin (Strelkov) – who had connections to the Russian secret service – on 12 April 2014. There was no military action prior to this act of war conducted by Russian citizens. After that Russian-backed separatists proclaimed, of two quasi-state entities, the 'DPR' (Donetsk People's Republic) and the 'LPR' (Luhansk People's Republic). The first government of the 'DPR' was led from May 2014 by Russian citizen and pro-Putin politician Aleksandr Borodai, currently a member of the Russian Duma ('United Russia' faction). In the other part of the Donbas, the first 'governor' of the 'LPR', in April 2014, was another Russian citizen and politician Valery Bolotov. Following this, the Ukrainian government launched an Anti-Terrorist Operation (ATO). 'By August 2014, pro-Russian fighters were on the verge of defeat and they were saved only by the invasion by regular Russian troops which led to the occupation of one-third of the Donbas' (Haran, Yakovlyev, & Zolkina, 2019, p. 6). As a result of this invasion, facing heavy losses, the Ukrainian government was forced to call for international negotiations to end the war over the Donbas. In August 2014, with mediation by the leaders of France and Germany, the Minsk

---

[4] For more on the religious landscape of Ukraine and its religious pluralism, see https://harvard-cga.maps.arcgis.com/apps/MapSeries/index.html?appid=9d7160c9e77a4f7bbd0384fe60eb3e2a.

Protocol was signed by the Trilateral Contact Group on Ukraine, which included Ukraine, the Russian Federation, and the Organization for Security and Co-operation in Europe [OSCE]); the protocol did not recognise the status of the two quasi-state entities.

This ceasefire did not last long. On 12 February 2015, after many long negotiations between the leaders of France, Germany, Russia, and Ukraine, a 'package of measures for the implementation of the Minsk agreements' ('Minsk II') was signed by the Trilateral Contact Group on Ukraine. Though it did not manage to achieve a stable ceasefire, it managed to de-escalate the situation substantially. Minsk II froze the status of the 'DPR' and the 'LPR' in the occupied parts of the Donetsk and Luhansk regions, and thus changed the character of the conflict from intense to protracted. The two quasi-state entities covered one-third of the Donbas territory, which was home to more than half of its pre-war population: around 6.5 million people. Altogether, some 3.5 million Donbas inhabitants found themselves living in temporarily occupied territories. While religious intolerance and political and physical persecutions were no less important factors pushing the inhabitants of the Donbas to leave the region, the major cause for their mass escape was military destruction.

1.2.4 The Directions of Conflict-Driven Displacement Flows

By the end of 2015, the number of officially registered IDPs who had fled from both Crimea and the Donbas to other regions in Ukraine, reached its peak (GRID, 2016). As of December 2015, in the countries that have common borders with Ukraine, such as Russia, Belarus, Poland, Slovakia, Hungary, and Moldova, there were 388,690 Ukrainians seeking refuge, and 730,100 Ukrainians seeking other forms of legal stay. In subsequent years, after the conflict had de-escalated and a temporary ceasefire was achieved following the Minsk I and Minsk II Agreements, the number of officially registered IDPs and asylum-seeking applicants gradually decreased. In December 2021, state and international agencies had registered close to 1.5 million IDPs (Ministerstvo Sotsialnoi Polityky Ukrainy, 2021) and 50,000 refugees – mostly in neighbouring countries (UNCHR, 2021). Altogether, some 2.4 million inhabitants of Crimea and 3.5 million inhabitants of the occupied territories of the Donbas found themselves behind the new dividing lines. Escaping from political and physical persecution or military hostilities, a part of the Crimean and Donbas population fled to other regions of Ukraine (1.8 million people) (GRID, 2016), to Russia (over 1 million) (UNHCR, 2016), or to other neighbouring countries.

The Ukrainian state was extremely slow in recognising the scope of the problem. After the beginning of the military conflict, people from the territories

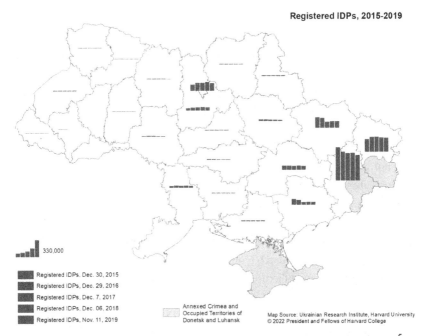

Map 1 Number of officially registered IDPs in each *oblast*, 2015–2019[5]

who were engulfed in the war or were in occupied Crimea received almost no support from the government to assist them in their relocation. Most people moved themselves and had to rely on their own resources, or they were helped by local activists from the receiving communities. This, to a great extent, defines the pattern of IDP resettlement. As one can see from Map 1, there are visible regional disproportions in the numbers of IDPs who resettled within Ukraine. Before 2022, areas of the Donbas controlled by the Ukrainian government accounted for over 55 per cent of all registered IDPs. After 2014 a quarter of Mariupol's population were IDPs, while the two neighbouring regions of Kharkiv and Zaporizhzhia hosted another 18–20 per cent and the capital city of Kyiv hosted 8–10 per cent. The majority of IDPs were concentrated in big cities.

There are many reasons that explain such disproportionate numbers (for a more detailed account, see Mikheieva & Sereda 2015) – among them are the scarcity of resources, limited experience with cross-regional mobility, the Ukrainian economy and the job market structure, the need to stay close to home (to care for family members who were unable to move, to take care of their property or the possibility to commute across the contact line), the silencing of urban and professional identities – especially for the IDPs from the

---

[5] *Map Source*: Harvard Ukrainian Research Institute (HURI) open online project, available at: https://gis.huri.harvard.edu/donbas-and-crimea-focus; *Data Source*: data provided by the UNHCR.

Confessional Belonging (6 most numerous groups), 2013

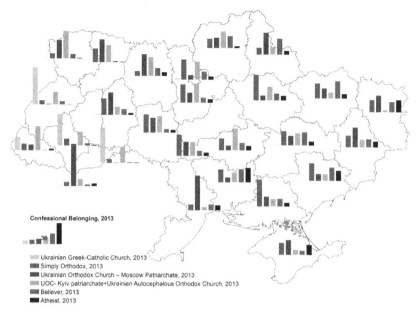

Confessional Belonging, 2013

36

Ukrainian Greek-Catholic Church, 2013
Simply Orthodox, 2013
Ukrainian Orthodox Church – Moscow Patriarchate, 2013
UOC- Kyiv patriarchate+Ukrainian Autocephalous Orthodox Church, 2013
Believer, 2013
Atheist, 2013

Map 2 Ukraine's religious landscape. Question: 'To which church (religious community, confession) do you belong?' (percentage of respondents, six most numerous groups, 2013)[6]

Donbas (Sereda, 2020) and, in a fewer number of cases, the religious or lingual landscapes of the country or cross-regional stereotypes (Maps 2 and 3). The specifics of conflict-driven migration abroad will be discussed in the following section.

The events described earlier, with their concomitant dislocation of people, have contributed to active reflections on who belongs to Ukrainian society and to the (re)articulation of the key markers that define one's sense of belonging. Opinion polls show that Ukrainians are demonstrating growing support for a political understanding of the nation. But at the same time, in its propaganda wars and disinformation campaigns, Russia has used arguments about persecution of Russian speakers as a pretext for occupying and annexing Ukrainian territories and has actively exploited certain historical myths and identity markers. Moreover, there is an intensive political and academic debate about the nature of the Donbas conflict. The dominant interpretation of the conflict is that it was an identity war – with polarised identities and memory projects being major factors in the escalation of the conflict (Matveeva, 2016; De Cordier,

---

[6] *Source*: illustrated by author.

Languages Spoken At Home, 2013, %

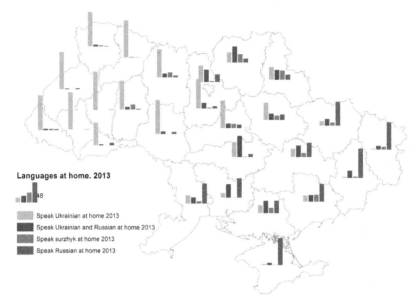

Map 3 Ukraine's lingual landscape. Main languages spoken at home
(percentage of respondents, 2013)[7]

2017). In my research, and with two decades of studying the region, I argue that such an interpretation considerably misrepresents and oversimplifies the conflict. The evidence that I have found in my fieldwork leads to more complex.

1.2.5 Russia's Full-Scale Aggression and a New Wave of Displacement

When in 2022 Russia attacked Ukraine, this was a continuation of the intervention in 2014 and a culmination of the hostilities perpetrated since then. From early 2021 Russia gradually built up a massive military presence along the Russian and Belarus borders with Ukraine. After failed attempts by the international community at de-escalation, on 21 February 2022 Russia officially recognised the quasi-state entities 'the Donetsk People's Republic' and 'the Luhansk People's Republic'. This was then used as a pretext to openly send Russian troops into the separatist-controlled territories. Three days later, Vladimir Putin launched an attack on Ukraine in an attempt to destroy the state. At first, Russian missiles exploded in all parts of the country. Putin appeared on television and announced

---

[7] *Source*: illustrated by author.

the beginning of a 'special military operation' in Ukraine, which in reality was Russia's full-scale invasion on a sovereign country. In his address, he lamented the dissolution of the Soviet Union, announced that old treaties and agreements were no longer effective ('[leading] to a redivision of the world, and the norms of international law that developed by that time – and the most important of them, the fundamental norms that were adopted following World War II (WWII)') and questioned Ukraine's right to exist, calling it 'our historical land' where a hostile 'anti-Russia' is taking shape.[8]

Regions that came under immediate attack were the most industrialised and urbanised parts of the country (see Map 4), resulting in a massive wave of displacement. According to the United Nations High Commissioner for Refugees' (UNHCR's) estimation, approximately one-third of Ukrainians have been forced to leave their homes and some 13 million people are estimated to be stranded in affected areas or unable to leave (UNHCR, 2022). International refugee organisations unanimously described this new wave of Ukrainian displacement as

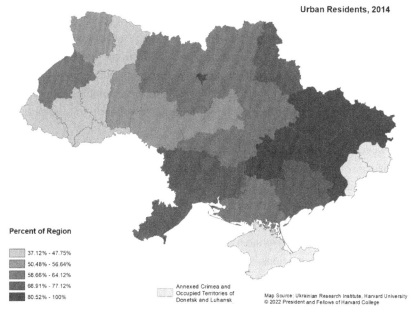

Map 4 Urban residents (percentage of region/*oblast*)[9]

---

[8] Vladimir Putin. *Address by the President of the Russian Federation*, 24 February 2022, available at: http://en.kremlin.ru/events/president/news/67843, accessed 03 October 2022.

[9] *Map Source*: Harvard Ukrainian Research Institute (HURI) open online project, available at: https://gis.huri.harvard.edu/donbas-and-crimea-focus; *Data Source*: data provided by the State Statistics Service of Ukraine.

the largest human displacement crisis in the world today; it has been unprecedented in the number of people displaced within such a short amount of time.

As of 27 September 2022, the European Commission of Migration and Home Affairs reported 7 million IDP (among which are 3 million children) and 11 million entries into the EU from Ukraine and Moldova out of which 9.6 million entries were by Ukrainian nationals. However, only 4.3 million registered for Temporary Protection in the EU and only 26,200 submitted asylum applications (European Commission, 2022). People were moving in chain steps – from more dangerous places to a safer one replacing those who left and were further ahead. If one compares Map 1 with the map of current military actions, it is evident that the majority of the IDPs who resettled after 2014 were now, for the second time, caught in the centre of military operations. For many of them this would mean being subjected to a double (and in some case triple) displacement. In 2014–2015 many stayed in the proximity of the temporarily occupied territories because of a lack of resources to move further (Map 1). Therefore, the second displacement became even more challenging. In early March, the biggest West Ukrainian city, Lviv, accommodated 250,000 displaced people and another 50,000 who were coming to the city daily before continuing their journey to the nearest border crossing to Poland. According to the Polish border control data, between 24 February and 25 April, the Polish-Ukrainian border was crossed by 2.944 million Ukrainian refugees. The situation in other countries neighbouring Ukraine was comparable to these numbers. This wave of displacement required enormous mobilisation and solidarity on the side of the receiving societies.

However, war and displacement have not only transformed the everyday experiences of those fleeing, they have also radically altered discussions about memory, basic values, and the politics of identity in the region (with some issues becoming less important or irrelevant and others becoming even more salient, such as the decommunisation and decolonisation processes). Once again, experiences and myths surrounding the Second World War became the nodal point of historical discussions – there were clashing representations of the war presented through both mass propaganda and through official discourses. Understanding of these mechanisms is important as the massive cross-border migration of displaced Ukrainians has become the subject of political debates that expose anxieties and concerns around identities, hierarchies of belonging, and historical memory in Ukraine and in the wider region. My research shows that historical memory might become an important factor that plays a role in processes of social inclusion and exclusion, stereotypisation, and othering. Early reports analysing the specifics of Ukrainian refugees' adaptation to neighbouring countries indicate that the post-Soviet diasporas play an important role in their accommodation (Isański et al., 2022; Soliman et al., 2022). At the same time, media reports alert us to aggression against Ukrainian refugees (e.g., there was an attempted arson attack on a shelter and nursery hosting Ukrainian refugees in Leipzig).[10] A survey conducted recently among displaced Ukrainians in Germany shows that almost a quarter of respondents admitted experiencing discrimination from the post-Soviet Russian-speaking diaspora and only 5 per cent from other national groups (Soliman et al., 2022). Therefore, the governments of receiving countries should pay more attention to the potential for conflict with other collective identities where attitudes towards the past can be triggered by propaganda outlets. These governments should consider conflict-prevention measures.

2 Conflict and (Re)shaped Narratives of Belonging (National Identities, Linguistic Divisions, Historical Memory)

This section begins with a re-examination of the main causes of the Russia-Ukrainian conflict before and after 2022, especially how it was seen in the scholarly literature. The outbreak of war and displacement of large population groups can dramatically change the established landscape of social and national identities, hierarchies, and politics of belonging causing anxieties and concerns that lie at the heart of national identity and culture. I first offer a comparative perspective on the prevailing situation in Ukrainian society, particularly in the Donbas and Crimea, exploring identities, language practices, and attitudes to the past before and after 2014. Secondly, I share some preliminary reflections on the current effects of Russian aggression on Ukrainian society.

2.1 Discussion about the Origins of the Conflict

The origins of Russo-Ukrainian conflict have been extensively discussed in expert and academic communities over the last eight years and, for the most part, these origins have been attributed to foreign factors or geopolitical considerations, for example, the asymmetrical end of the Cold War with North Atlantic Treaty Organization's (NATO's) expansion (Mearsheimer, 2014; Sakwa, 2014). Authors' explanations vary from classical 'systems in conflict' – 'Deepening Russian-Western confrontations' (Hahn, 2018), to blaming post-Soviet economic inequalities and global military security challenges such as, 'The capitalist oligarchy that appropriated post-communist

---

[10] German police investigate attempted arson at a nursery hosting Ukrainian refugees. *Euronews,* 31 August 2022, available at: www.euronews.com/2022/08/31/german-police-investigate-attempted-arson-at-a-nursery-hosting-ukrainian-refugees, accessed 03 October 2022.

Ukraine's wealth by privatising old Soviet centres of power' (van der Pijl, 2018), 'Transnational insurgency' (Gomza, 2019) and 'Russia's use of different tactics of societal destabilisation and covert occupation as a part of its military and security doctrine to manage a regional security complex that is critical to both its identity and ability to retain great power status and the capability to act globally' (Malyarenko & Wolff, 2018). Clearly some authors were using the outdated Cold War explanatory framework based on the concept of continuing conflict between 'two great powers': Russia and the West. However, this explanation appears to be unsuitable for understanding the real character of the Russian intervention in 2014. Others pointed to domestic factors (Kuzio, 2015; Yekelchyk, 2015; Wilson, 2016; Haran, Yakovlyev, & Zolkina, 2019), although there is still little agreement about the main domestic conflict-provoking factors. One group (Matveeva, 2016; Zhukov, 2016) is blamed for using 'economic determinism' as the main explanatory framework (Mykhnenko, 2020); others (Kuzio, 2015; Wilson, 2016; De Cordier, 2017) for exploiting 'the identity- and history-centred essentialist interpretations' (Portnov, 2015). However, identity-based explanations prevailed, especially in the media discourse: 'Of all international news items on the conflict published in its first year, 55 per cent mentioned Russian ethnicity, language or military support, while just 23 per cent mentioned any economic issues' (Zhukov, 2016, p. 2). With the recent escalation caused by Russia's concentration of military forces on Ukraine's borders and later Russia's invasion of Ukraine, the narratives about the asymmetrical end of the Cold War and Ukraine being the ground of civilisational wars actively entered media outlets again.

Attribution of causes influences the terminology that is applied to label the conflict and its character (e.g., international 'Russian aggression', 'Russian invasion', 'Russian-Ukrainian war', or internal 'civil war', 'civil conflict'). Andriy Zayarnyuk (2022) points to 'the trope of the "Ukrainian crisis" instead of "Russia's war," as the most dubious explanatory framework for understanding the revanchist Russian intervention of 2014'. How conflict is understood and described influences what measures for conflict resolution are proposed (for a detailed analysis of the narratives used to describe the conflict in Western academia and think-tank communities, see Koval et al., 2022), Moreover, it also influences how the fleeing population is portrayed in the media and treated by the receiving communities. For example, if conflict is portrayed as a civil war, it might reinforce the bias that people escaping from those regions subscribe to separatist views and should not be trusted or welcomed.

2.1.1 Economy-Based Explanations

In 2014 Russia's 'justification' of its actions in Crimea was mostly based on historical arguments and arguments regarding identity. Economy-based arguments were almost never used to justify the annexation. However, they are often applied to explain the crisis in the Donbas. Among the key arguments is the idea of fear that the region's strong economic ties with Russia would be broken if Ukraine signed the EU–Ukraine Association Agreement. It was argued that the population was afraid that this would produce a new shock to the local economy and labour market. In the post-Perestroika period, the Donbas struggled to keep up old economic ties and became export-oriented: 'As of 2014, some 80 per cent of production in the Donbas went to export, with Russia as the leading destination' (Zhukov, 2016, p. 4). The local government's strategy to increase subsidies has only exacerbated socio-economic problems and could not solve the issue of 'dying' mono-industrial cities. This structural-economic discrepancy as Yuri Zhukov (2016) argued later played a role in pro-separatist insurgency. In areas where the 'opportunity costs of insurgency' were low, such as in 'dying' mono-cities or in manufacturing towns which were more exposed to trade shocks with Russia, the risk of armed conflict was greater overall and separatist violence was more frequent. However, critics (Portnov, 2015; Mykhnenko, 2020;) say that Zhukov's argument might account for some local mobilisation trends but could not explain the outbreak of military hostilities without considering international factors: the question of the proliferation of weapons and the role of Ukrainian oligarchs based in the Donbas. A socio-economic explanatory model also could not explain why pro-separatist protests did not start earlier with the beginning of the Russia-Ukraine trade war in July 2013 (Popescu, 2013) or why regions adjacent to the Donbas with similar economic structures (and problems) did not follow the same course.

Besides, the future prosperity of the region was not only associated with Russia. In 2012 Donetsk was a host city of the 2012 European Football Championship, which brought investment and infrastructure changes to the region, and a newly built airport connected the Donbas with several European destinations. For many people 'the Donbas finally became Europe'. For them it was the highest point of the region's development, which also influenced their livelihood with many speaking of increased income, renovated or newly acquired apartments, and so on.

2.1.2 Identity-Based Explanations

Identity-based explanations of the crisis are often rooted in the external experts' perspectives on Ukraine's development post-independence. In the early 1990s, some scholars described this as a civilisational conflict between the Orthodox and the Catholic worlds (Huntington, 1993) or through the stereotypical binary division of ethnic-cultural versus civic nationalism (Wilson, 1995), which follow ethno-linguistic and regional lines. Moreover, the differences in remembering and interpreting some key historical events, described as a competition between Ukrainian nationalists and Soviet models of the past were often identified as the main dividing lines within Ukrainian society (Wilson, 1995). This simplified image of 'two Ukraines' was picked up by the media and politicians both within and outside the country, and for years it became a key approach in the assessment of Ukraine's transformations and political conflicts. Though many external and internal experts warned against such a simplified approach to Ukraine's regionalism (Sereda, 2002; Barrington & Herron, 2004; Schmid & Myshlovska, 2019), this stereotypical view prevailed, and with the start of the Euromaidan protests, especially after the outbreak of the military conflict, immediately resurfaced. Similar arguments were often used by the pro-Russian propaganda outlets portraying the conflict as between two worlds or superpowers, and presenting Ukraine as manipulated by the USA/EU therefore denying Ukraine's autonomy and the people's political choice. These narratives were internalised by the local population in the temporarily occupied territories. Interviewed IDPs from the Donbas often described the conflict as encouraged from above by global superpowers, and part of a political-economic war between the Kremlin and USA/EU or a cultural-religious confrontation between the Orthodox and Catholic worlds. In the majority of cases, they denied their own agency in the conflict and described their localities as suddenly turning into the site of violent conflict (as one respondent described, 'There is a longstanding history of the confrontation between these two superpowers, and we just happened to be in the wrong place').

It is important to bear in mind that the success of peacebuilding and decisions on acceptable ways for conflict resolution very much depend on how the society in conflict and the international community view the conflict itself. Knowledge is vital for all parties involved in a peace-making process enabling them to address concrete challenges and provide relevant peacekeeping solutions. A recent study by Koval et al. (2022), which reviewed publications from the United States, the United Kingdom, Germany, France, Italy, Greece, and Poland explaining the situation in Ukraine, showed that narratives about Ukraine as a battlefield between Russia and the West are still very much present in some of the international scholars' policy reports attributing responsibility for the ongoing conflict. This approach also often 'blames the Ukrainian government and Ukrainian ethno-nationalism for developments in Crimea and the Donbas', for repressing Russian speakers, and points to the irreconcilable identity differences between Kyiv and/or western Ukraine on the one hand and the regions under consideration (Haran, 2019; Koval et al., 2022), on the other. The data from the 'Region, Nation, and Beyond' survey give us an opportunity to test the veracity of these arguments.

National Self-Identification and Linguistic Divisions

This survey, conducted in March 2013, asked respondents about their nationality according to their own description, native language, and the language they use at home. Table 1 (Appendix 3) illustrates the distribution of answers in Crimea and the Donbas. It shows that Crimea was the only region in Ukraine where a majority self-identified as Russians (57 per cent). In the Donbas the proportion of those who described themselves as Ukrainians was higher than indicated in the last census. A year prior to the outbreak of the military conflict three-quarters of the inhabitants of Donetsk *oblast* and two-thirds of Luhansk described themselves as Ukrainians. However, only 3 per cent in both regions claimed that they use Ukrainian in their everyday interactions at home. This indicates that ethnic and linguistic lines do not correspond.

The simple measurement of respondents' self-identification tells us nothing about the strength or importance of this identification at the personal level or what it means to be X and the key markers of inclusion and exclusion. An individual might self-categorise as X by nationality, but in everyday life feel very little attachment to that identity. In contrast, it might be the most important dimension of someone's identity. It is crucial to understand what the importance of national identity is when compared to other social and territorial identities for the inhabitants of both regions, compared to those who live in other parts of the country. Table 2 (Appendix 3) presents a comparison of mean values for each listed identity[11] in 2013 for Crimea, as well as the Donetsk and Luhansk and six other neighbouring regions. It demonstrates that in the Donbas and Crimea the most important factors were generational followed by local/regional factors, and, in Crimea, professional factors. The strength of Crimea's local identity was above average when compared to the rest of the country, but comparable to that of neighbouring *oblasts*. The mean value of the Donbas' local identity was lower than those of its immediate neighbours. However, in both regions local/regional identities were stronger than national identities. The importance of Russian and East Slavic identities for the inhabitants of both regions were above the national and regional mean, but, in the Donbas, lower than the importance of

---

[11] Respondents were asked to measure the importance of ten prelisted identities (local, regional, national and transnational (European and East Slavic), class, professional, generational, religious) on a 5-point scale, where 1 is 'definitely not important' and 5 'very important.'

Ukrainian identity.[12] For the inhabitants of Crimea, Russian and Ukrainian identities were equally important. Those outcomes confirm the results of the 2010 Crimean study which showed that the peninsula's sense of territorial/ regional identity and belonging were primarily tied to Crimea itself, while their Ukrainian or Russian ethnic affiliations were generally less salient and less articulated. Simultaneously, neither Crimea, nor the Donbas, demonstrated salient pro-Russian sentiments. When asked to rate markers of their 'Ukrainianness',[13] inhabitants of both regions prioritised the political concept of belonging to the nation – 'to feel Ukrainian' and 'to respect Ukrainian political institutions and law'. The third most important marker in Crimea was 'to have Ukrainian citizenship' and for those in the Donbas it was 'to live in Ukraine for most of one's life'.

Another interesting aspect of the analysis of national belonging would be to compare to what extent respondents who self-identified as Russians felt that Ukrainian identity is also important to them and vice versa. Table 3 (Appendix 3) illustrates the regional distribution of respondents' attitudes to Ukrainian and Russian identity in 2013 according to their self-identification as Russian or Ukrainian. An important outcome of the comparison is that the significance of Ukrainian identity to those who self-identified as Russians in both regions was above the mean value. Similarly Russian identity was important to those respondents who self-categorised as Ukrainians; in fact, it was almost at the same level. Therefore, Ukrainians and Russians in Crimea and the Donbas cannot be described as two separate antagonistic national groups, but rather as strongly inter-twined and mutually inclusive groups with blurred lines between group boundaries. This results in an important implication – it gives us a very different perspective to that presented by the Russian media and some international experts on the processes of identity building that were taking place in Crimea and in the Donbas region before 2014. Both regions had a strong sense of local/regional identity, but in terms of national self-identification the absolute majority of the inhabitants of the Donbas and Crimea saw themselves as a part of a Ukrainian political project.

Ukraine's political life before 2014 was marked by three revolutions – in 1990 ('Revolution on Granite'), 2004 ('Orange Revolution'), and 2013 ('Euromaidan or Revolution of Dignity') – which prevented the establishment

---

[12] Russian in Donetsk *oblast* = 2.88 and Luhask = 3.31; in Ukrainian in Donetsk *oblast* = 3.95, Luhansk = 3.65; in Crimea Russian = 3.76 and Ukrainian = 3.71.

[13] (1) Be born in Ukraine, (2) Have Ukrainian citizenship, (3) Live in Ukraine for most of one's life, (4) Speak Ukrainian, (5) Respect Ukrainian political institutions and law, (6) Feel Ukrainian, (7) Have Ukrainian origin.

of an authoritarian regime and preserved political pluralism in the country. Regionalism was massively weaponised in Ukrainian political life after 1991. Yet, since 2014 all elections show that regional cleavages are not a crucial factor any longer. New solidarities were built across regional, ethnic, linguistic, or religious lines. Another important change was enormous growth in civil society activism and self-aid support networks as a response to the war and dislocation.

The current President Volodymyr Zelensky – the sixth president in a row – was elected at internationally recognised elections with support of 73 per cent. His electoral campaign was based on a particular kind of populism free of anti-liberal, nationalistic, or right-wing rhetoric. He came to power under the slogan of making peace and made many steps in this direction – he called for the Normandy group meeting, withdrew military forces, and created several demili-tarisation zones along the demarcation line in the Donbas. In his famous New Year's speech in December 2020, he argued for an inclusive historic and linguistic policy saying, 'It does not matter who you are'.[14]

However, Putin portrays Ukraine as an artificial state where a lawless regime discriminates Russians, totally ignoring all democratic political processes in the country. In his aggressive nationalist rhetoric, all anti-Kremlin activities were labelled as 'Nazism'.

As many commentators claim,[15] accusing Zelensky of Nazism is absurd because he himself is a descendant of a Holocaust survivor. What stands behind Putin's rhetoric is not the desire to help alleged victims of the so-called Ukrainian regime, but an attempt to destroy the Ukrainian democratic system, perceived as a threat to his authoritarian regime. In fact, the Russian state-owned news agency RIA Novosti openly published a plan of how to reshape people's identity by force,[16] which is rooted in the nineteenth-century imperial-istic and nationalistic imagination (Zayarnyuk and Sereda, 2022) that deprives people and their choices and voices.

Shortly after the outbreak of a full-scale war, Putin's rhetoric about fighting with 'Ukrainian Nazis' became evidently absurd. Despite his mantras about

---

[14] Zelensky, V. Davayte kozhen chesno vidpovist' na vazhlyve pytannya: khto ya? Novorichne pryvitannya prezydenta Zelens'koho. *TSN,* 31 December 2019, available at: https://tsn.ua/politika/davayte-kozhen-chesno-vidpovist-na-vazhlive-pitannya-hto-ya-novorichne-privitannya-prezidenta-zelenskogo-1468050.html, accessed 23 September 2022.

[15] Veidlinger, J. (2022). Putin's claim to rid Ukraine of Nazis is especially absurd given its history. *The Conversation*, 26 February, available at: http://theconversation.com/putins-claim-to-rid-ukraine-of-nazis-is-especially-absurd-given-its-history-177959, accessed 12 September 2022.

[16] See the programmatic text published by the Russian state-owned news agency RIA Novosti '*What Russian should do with Ukrainians*?' published by Timofey Sergeytsev on 6 April 2022. Translation available at: https://medium.com/@kravchenko_mm/what-should-russia-do-with-ukraine-translation-of-a-propaganda-article-by-a-russian-journalist-a3e92e3cb64, accessed 30 September 2022.

the denazification of the Ukrainian regime, the main regions under attack, and the cities subjected to the heaviest shelling, are those with the highest share of the Russian-speaking population (see Map 3). At the same time, their inhabitants demonstrate active anti-Russian resilience, civic cohesion, and self-aid networks.

However, the continual Russian intervention that led to the militarisation of the conflict in 2014 and the resulting displacement of millions of Ukrainians remained largely unnoticed by international observers. The annexation of the territories followed by the outbreak of war and displacement of large population groups stimulated an unprecedented wave of social mobilisation and transformed the established landscape of social and national identities (as discussed earlier) as well as hierarchies and politics of belonging. Peter Gatrell (1999) argues that the new category of 'refugee' suddenly created by the war might become an important social category and a factor of identity in itself. Described processes can be attributed not only to the displaced (both internally and cross-border) but also to the society in conflict and the receiving communities. War and displacement provoke questions such as, who is 'us' (or in the case of cross-border displacement questions about solidarity and belonging, with some groups seen to belong more, and therefore to deserve more, than others) causing anxieties and concerns that lie at the heart of national identity as well as the transformation of hierarchies of belonging.

The academic literature argues that war, or territorial conflict, creates incentives for unity against rivals, and this provokes strong nationalistic responses among the citizenry (Vasquez, 2009). Our research shows that Russia's annexation of Crimea and its military operations in the Donbas have rekindled Ukrainian nationalism, although unpredictably. Opinion polls from 2015 onwards show that Ukrainians demonstrate a growing support for the nation as a political entity. Comparative ranking of the importance attributed by Ukrainian citizens to the listed markers of national identity (representing 'ethnic/cultural' or 'political' types of nationalism) in 2013 and 2015[17] illustrates that by 2015, the group of markers representing the 'political/civil' type of national identification appeared to be increasingly gaining importance. The Social Cohesion and Reconciliation (SCORE, 2022) longitudinal study of social cohesion, national attachment, and inclusive identification in Ukraine came to a similar conclusion that 'pluralistic Ukrainian identity and sense of belonging to the country enjoyed high support in Ukraine. There were no significant differences between western and eastern *oblasts* or based on spoken language (Russian or Ukrainian)'.

---

[17] *Identities and Regionalism*, available at: https://infogram.com/f85d270b-0c96-40ea-ad10-ca859022d2e1, accessed 23 December 2021.

Consequently, one can conclude that contrary to the picture described by Russian propaganda, Euromaidan and the later tragic events have had a positive impact on the feeling of Ukrainian statehood and reduced ethnocentric attitudes. Among other markers, the importance of speaking Ukrainian also lost its significance. What's more, markers emphasising the importance of citizenship practices to Ukrainian identity[18] appeared to be highly important and relevant for respondents across Ukraine, and specifically for the Donbas region. Similar results were reported by Volodymyr Kulyk (2016) and Olexyi Haran et al. (2019). The interconnectedness of the Donbas and Crimea with other regions has acquired critical political importance both at the level of daily interactions between the IDPs and their new communities and at the level of national discourse. Mottos like 'Donbas is Ukraine' and 'Crimea is Ukraine' became increasingly visible in public spaces and media all over the country.

A comparison of pre- and post-Euromaidan hierarchies of belonging shows that Ukrainian society was going through a positive redefinition of social distance towards almost all ethnic groups except for Russians who, before 2014, were perceived as one of the 'closest' ethnic groups and after 2014 experienced the most dramatic shift in attitudes (Sereda, 2020; SCORE, 2022). At the same time, social distancing towards the displaced – IDPs from Crimea and the Donbas – was low. Both groups were perceived as belonging to Ukrainian society. However, respondents felt somewhat threatened by pro-Russian oriented people living in the temporarily occupied territories, and people supporting the separation of those territories (SCORE, 2022).

The sociological surveys conducted in Ukraine in 2022 (Rating, 2022; KIIS, 2022) show that even after Russia's full-scale aggression, the 'political/civil' type of national identification and the importance of civic activism became even stronger (self-identification as a 'Ukrainian citizen' on a 10-point scale grew from 7.9 in August 2021 to 9.8 in April 2022). There were no visible shifts in defining Ukrainian or Russian as the respondents' native language, but a visible shift in declared usage of the Ukrainian language in media consumption and in public. There was a public controversy over legislation promoting the use of Ukrainian language, but language was not a factor in political mobilisation any longer.

An analysis of the population's attitudes towards the new wave of displacement in Ukraine, conducted in May 2022, demonstrates their full support: 61 per cent of respondents answered that people in their locality have a 'positive-compassionate' attitude and another 25 per cent claimed that they are treated 'similarly to any other dweller' (InfoSapience, 2022). Only

---

[18] Be ready to defend Ukraine; help other Ukrainians; participate actively in civic life; consider Ukrainians the citizens of all ethnic origin.

5 per cent noted negative attitudes and explained them as resulting from IDPs' demonstrative leisure practices during a time of war. Language as a factor in negative stereotyping was named by only 2 per cent of respondents. Macro-level analysis demonstrates that, starting from 2014 and inspired by the war-related shocks, Ukrainian society manifests support for a pluralistic understanding of Ukrainian identity and inclusive attitudes towards different social groups including IDPs.

Historical Memory

Disagreements about historical events are regularly noted as another cause of identity-based explanations of the conflict. This implies that separatist sentiments were seeded in the Donbas and Crimean communities because they 'were forced to accept an interpretation of history and cultural symbols that they did not share, and which were alien to them' (Matveeva, 2016).

Our analysis of changes in the sphere of mnemonic practices and historical memory discourses demonstrates that the period prior to 2014 (Leibich, Myshlovska, & Sereda, 2019) can be characterised by constant shifts in the official historical narrative, and a visible plurality of ideas of the past that were articulated and instrumentalised by the ruling elites. Soviet Ukrainian, Ukrainian national, and Russian imperial representations of the past, as well as victimisation narratives, were used variously by the changing Ukrainian leadership to forge new senses of belonging. Therefore, the simplified concept of conflict between the Soviet and post-Soviet (colonial and post-colonial) narratives and the replacement of the former by the latter misrepresents key aspects of the process. Instead, I propose to see post-Soviet changes in the Ukrainian historical memory as several attempts by conflicting elites to rearticulate some outdated markers, and to create a new hybrid version to achieve social harmony in a polarised society, or, alternatively, to politicise some elements of the past. In certain periods, censorship and silence were prioritised; in other periods there was limited and highly guided discussion on conflicting pasts.

As a rule, those historical models peacefully coexisted (the mechanism of segregation of memory) or, even more often, merged into ambivalent combinations of historical narratives on a local level. Grassroots memorialisation activism was limited. Over the last twenty years the Soviet model was successfully incorporated into the Ukrainian meta-narratives, and both discourses have become intertwined in all regions of Ukraine, except in some western parts and parts of Kyiv. Inhabitants of the rest of Ukraine did not demonstrate clear-cut support for any particular model of Ukraine's past. Their attitudes were more multi-layered as Soviet Ukrainian, Russian Imperial, Ukrainian-centred, and other representations of the past coexist in their areas to different degrees. It is important to note that neither the Donbas nor Crimea demonstrated any strong differentiation in their attitudes towards the past from the neighbouring *oblasts*. The continued celebration of Victory Day[19] and other Soviet holidays across most regions of the country serve as an example (Maps 5 and 6).

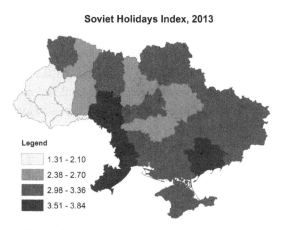

Soviet Holidays Index, 2013

Legend
- 1.31 - 2.10
- 2.38 - 2.70
- 2.98 - 3.36
- 3.51 - 3.84

Map 5 Soviet holidays index (mean value of the index created as a sum of five ex-Soviet holidays: February 23rd, March 8th, May Day, Victory Day, and Great October Revolution Day, 2013)[20]

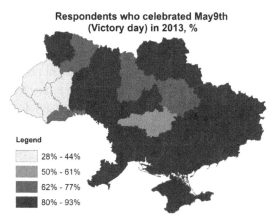

Respondents who celebrated May9th (Victory day) in 2013, %

Legend
- 28% - 44%
- 50% - 61%
- 62% - 77%
- 80% - 93%

Map 6 Percentage of respondents in each *oblast* who celebrated May 9th (Victory Day) in 2013[21]

---

[19] 9th of May – the myth of the Great Patriotic War was the cultural foundation of the 'new historical community of Soviet people' (for a detailed discussion, see Fedor, Lewis, & Zhurzhenko, 2017).
[20] *Source*: illustrated by author [21] *Source*: illustrated by author.

The Euromaidan protests prompted an active revision of past, aiming to legitimise one side and de-legitimise the other. In public spaces it resulted, first of all, in the so-called 'Leninfall'. The spontaneous process of symbolic recodification of urban and rural spaces changed the nation's character after the acceptance of the controversial decommunisation laws by the Supreme Council of Ukraine in April 2015. This intensified the process of removing symbolic Soviet monuments and names and strengthened the role of the state in that process. Amongst other things, the law established a six-month period for the removal of all monuments to Lenin and leaders of the Communist regime as well as Communist-related names from the names of toponyms. After the five years of decommunisation, over 51,000 toponyms had their names changed (among them over 1,000 settlements) and close to 2,500 monuments were dismantled (including over 1,300 monuments to Lenin).[22] However, changes in Ukrainians' attitudes towards the renaming of toponyms were not so fast. In March 2013, according to the 'Region, Nation and Beyond' survey, 18 per cent of respondents supported the renaming and 48 per cent were opposed. In 2020 similar results were reported: where only 30 per cent of Ukrainians supported the renaming, 44 per cent opposed it. The percentage of supporters increased by 12 per cent, while the number of those who opposed remained practically the same.[23]

Moreover, immediately after the Euromaidan, public activism reached its peak and spontaneous local grassroots initiatives emerged that sought the creation of a new heroic cult (of Euromaidan victims called the Heavenly Hundred). Very soon, this heroic narrative developed into a new more powerful one associated with the armed conflict in the Donbas. Opinion polls demonstrate that for the first time in Ukraine's recent history, a new cult of heroes had emerged, who were supported by an overwhelming majority (three-quarters) of respondents in practically all regions of Ukraine. The Russian-Ukrainian war directly affected much wider circles of Ukrainian society (Sereda, 2016). Ukrainian soldiers killed in the war represented all possible social strata and regions of Ukraine. This cult was accompanied by a wave of spontaneous commemorations 'from below' often in the form of 'public memorials' or improvised exhibitions created by local residents in honour of the defenders of Ukrainian independence and territorial integrity from Russia (Anti-Terroristic Operation (ATO) soldiers). In many areas,

---

[22] Over the years of decommunisation, more than 1,300 monuments to Lenin were dismantled in Ukraine. *Ukrinform*, 16 July 2020, available at: www.ukrinform.ua/rubric-society/3064494-za-sroki-dekomunizacii-v-ukraini-demontuvali-bils-ak-1300-pamatnikiv-leninu.html, accessed 3 September 2021.

[23] Shostyi Rik Dekomunizatsii: Pidsumky ta Prohnozy, 16 July 2020, available at : https://dif.org.ua/article/shostiy-rik-dekomunizatsii-stavlennya-naselennya-do-zaboroni-simvoliv-totalitarnogo-minulogo, accessed 3 September 2021.

those new commemoration sites are intertwined with the cults of fallen soldiers of the Soviet Afghan or the Great Patriotic Wars.

Post-Euromaidan Ukraine is undergoing an intensive process of (re)articulating the past and (re)imagining mnemonic spaces. It is happening at all levels of society simultaneously and involves very diverse social actors, although it may vary in scope, content, and geographic localisation. Interestingly, Ukrainians are more willing to accept new cults of heroes as well as new holidays than the attempt to alter the meanings of existing Soviet ones. Changes of attitudes to already codified holidays, events, or personalities differ in scope. In general, as might be expected, the Soviet and Russian imperial representations of the past are gradually losing their support and Ukrainian representation is increasing, but there are regional variations. The turbulent events of the twentieth century and especially the Soviet myth of the 'Great Patriotic War' are at the core of remapping spaces of memory.

Moreover, society was actively challenged by transnational mnemonic discourses. On the one hand, further integration into the European community deepened the debates about conflictual and shameful pages in Ukraine's past; on the other, there remained a constant need to respond to the gradually escalating pro-Russian propaganda, which was highly mythologised and included a lot of historical argumentations. As Andriy Zayarnyuk (2022) stresses, 'History is absolutely central to the ideology that underpins Russia's genocidal war in Ukraine. Putin's justifications of Russian aggression have repeatedly resorted to history and purported historical arguments. Putin's decision to escalate the invasion was preceded by his infamous article "On the Historical Unity of Russians and Ukrainians." On the very eve of the invasion, he reiterated his denial of the existence of the Ukrainian nation, supporting it with references to the past'. The nodal points in Putin's ideology are the greatness of the 'Kyivan Rus' and the Soviet past – specifically the glorification of the Great Patriotic War. Putin's speeches reveal that his greatest imagined threat is the dissolution of the Soviet Union as one of the great powers ruling the world. Therefore, Ukraine's democratic aspirations undermine his aspirations of rebuilding it and are portrayed as an American, or the West's, plot to undermine 'mighty Russia' by imposing new values and identities.

3 Empowering the Disempowered: The Response of Civil Society to the State Governance of the Internally Displaced Population

Internal displacement governance is shaping new lines of social inclusion or exclusion through the production of multiple internal physical, symbolic, or bureaucratic borders and their impact on the IDPs' sense of belonging.

First, I will examine the emergence of new 'borders' as a consequence of the annexation of Crimea and the beginning of the war over the Donbas. I will explore how this new border control, as well as policies directed at the resettled population, produced new physical and symbolic lines of division within Ukrainian society. The emergence in 2014 of a new social group of internally displaced persons (IDPs) in Ukraine (or in the everyday media discourse: 'refugees' or 'migrants') also affected the established hierarchies of group affiliation in society. In Peter Gatrell's (1999) work on refugees during the First World War, he illustrates how the outbreak of war and the subsequent appearance of a new social group ('refugees') can dramatically change the established social landscape. Sometimes people see this category as artificial and imposed from above or, in other circumstances, it might suddenly become an important factor in identity and outweigh a person's previous statuses and identities. Moreover, the belonging of the displaced (internally or cross-border) is framed not only through borders, laws, and administrative policies – the state's symbolic power of nomination and categorisation – but also through attitudes present in society. Processes of (re)negotiating a sense of belonging triggered by the military conflict and subsequent displacement does not only involve the refugees (IDPs) but the receiving communities as well.

Later I demonstrate how a change of perspective from state and state-related institutions to civil society structures with regard to migration governance can help us to avoid paternalistic approaches of viewing the IDPs or refugees as passive aid recipients and spotlight their agency in the receiving communities. Moreover, it allows us to build new lines of inclusion and citizen solidarity through active engagement in various forms of activism, by strengthening the feeling of resilience and of belonging even in a spate of obstacles created by state.

3.1 IDPs and the Debates on Migration Governance

The literature on migration governance mostly focuses on transborder migration, and as a result IDPs are viewed as distinct from the other types of migrants because 'They are citizens of the country, who have moved (not for economic reasons) within and not across internationally recognised state boundaries and therefore entitled to the full rights of other citizens, as opposed to the limited rights granted to international migrants and refugees. The primary responsibility for fulfilling their rights falls on their own states, as opposed to transborder migration host states or the international community' (Koser, 2011, p. 210). Following the 'Guiding Principles on Internal Displacement' definition the IDPs are often treated as a separate category. Instead, I propose a wider understanding of the phenomenon as, when internal displacement is conflict-induced and does not result from ecological/technological disaster, the population is split between government-controlled areas (GCA) and temporarily occupied territories, creating legal situations and experiences comparable to cross-border migration. Moreover, it is rarely possible to contain the displaced within national borders and describe trajectories of their resettlement as unidirectional – as going from point A to point B. In official reports, one encounters established groups (IDPs or refugees), but these are rarely pure categories. A person can move within a country by registering his/her status as an IDP or avoiding it. Moreover, one can live some of the time as an IDP and some of the time as a displaced person abroad (documented or undocumented) or even return to the occupied territories. Within one family, individual members can have quite different statuses and trajectories. Against the backdrop of the increasing duration of the conflict the operational separation between refugees and IDPs can hardly be maintained.

Secondly, I want to stress the continuous 'invisibility' of IDPs in European migration research, which has mostly focused on a cross-border migration and immigrants and refugees coming to the region. Previously, the IDP phenomenon has been associated with the Global South, not with Eastern Europe. By 2016, Ukraine had the largest number of IDPs in Europe and the fifth largest in the world, yet European media did not consider Ukraine in their internal debates about the 'migrant threat' in their respective countries. In February 2022, after the onset of Russian aggression, the media have been mostly focused on refugees fleeing the country, but the critical situation and negative effects of that conflict on internal displacement within the country (currently estimated to amount to 7 million people) has received little attention once again.

Thirdly, when IDP or refugee governance is discussed, the main focus is on the provision of basic rights, socio-economic stability, and (if necessary) humanitarian aid to the displaced, along with institutional and political/normative order (often associated with state and international organisations as the key actors) responsible for the provision. Therefore, it overlooks the agency of those who migrated and their influence on the receiving communities.

All over the world, displaced people are often viewed as groups coping with the psychological consequences and humanitarian problems of resettlement. Moreover, the literature on people displaced within their own state (IDPs) is often framed in terms of their traumatic experiences (Grace & Mooney, 2009; Siriwardhana & Stewart, 2013), humanitarian issues and lack of legal freedoms (Mooney, 2001; Grace & Mooney, 2009; Koser, 2011; World Migration Report (WMR), 2020). In many publications the notion of 'IDPs' or 'refugees' is coupled with the terms 'problems' or 'humanitarian issues', further contributing to the rhetorical and visual fixation with them as a powerless and victimised group. More needs to be known about the conscious and productive efforts of displaced people to rebuild their lives in the new receiving communities as well as the response of the civil society in these receiving communities. A novel way of thinking about internal or cross-border displacement would involve the analysis of their inclusion into civil society networks and different non-formal means of citizen participation, allowing for quick and flexible responses to changing needs in different situations. Such interactions empower the displaced and give them experiences which show how it is possible to solve social problems with different levels of difficulty – from the local to the (trans) national – and assist with their adaptation. My study aims to change the perspective and examine the specifics of civic engagement using the Ukrainian IDPs as a case study. Thus, there might be some lessons to be learned from the national and international responses to the Ukrainian IDP/refugee crisis for the global governance of international migration studies.

Furthermore, integration policies are often narrowly defined by policymakers as the 'Rights and responsibilities for immigrants associated with their admission to the country' (Lutz, 2017, p. 6). They are often understood in terms of institutional provision of possibilities (be it at the level of the state or local communities) for better access to education, labour market, affordable housing and health services (as the core areas of concern), as well as civic and political involvement (European Union Action Plan, 2016; World Migration Report (WMR), 2020). The host society is often described as something homogeneous, and the immigrants as lacking knowledge or skills, and needing to learn the receiving community's way of life. For example, in the 'European Union Action Plan on Integration of the Third-Country Nationals' released in 2016,[24] integration is described as a two-way process, but mostly in terms of the binary opposition: 'we provide' and 'they are expected to embrace', hence, '[t]his dynamic two-way process on integration means not only *expecting* third-country nationals to embrace EU fundamental values and learn the host language but also *offering* them meaningful opportunities to participate in the economy and society of the Member State where they settle' (European Union Action Plan, 2016, p. 5). Lutz (2017) in his analysis of the logics of policy intervention in immigrant integration argues that integration policies, to a substantial degree, fall between assimilationist and multicultural approaches (for a detailed discussion of both, see Brubaker, 2001; Kymlicka, 2010). However, it could be argued that it is important to see the integrational processes

---

[24] *European Union Action Plan on Integration of the Third-Country Nationals* (2016), Strasbourg, 7 June 2016, available at: https://eur-lex.europa.eu/legal-content/EN/TXT/?uri=CELEX%3A52016DC0377&qid=1632298272980, accessed 2 September 2021.

associated with migration, not only as an outcome of policy intervention, but as an outcome of migrants' activities which make an impact and bring social change to the receiving communities.

Numerous studies from different parts of the world demonstrate that institutional provision of possibilities or incentives for the newcomers does not fully resolve the complex problem of the redefinition of identity and hierarchies of belonging for both the host community and those resettled there (Lubbers, Molina, & McCarty, 2007; Skey, 2014), sometimes echoed in heated political debates or social unrest. Along which lines do these debates, evoked by the influx of the refugees/IDPs, go? Steven Vertovec (2011) demonstrates that one of the key devices for constructing the national imagery in regard to migration is the conceptual triad *identities-borders-orders* ('IBO model'). He understands migration only as a cross-border phenomenon, and in so doing overlooks the phenomenon of IDPs, which is relevant for many societies.

In this section I use the case of Ukraine to show that the annexation of a country's territories or the outbreak of war unavoidably generates multiple physical, symbolic, and legal/bureaucratic borders within the society ('borders and orders') and leads to a redefinition of identities.

3.2 The State Response to Internal Displacement

After Russia's military seizure of Crimea, the peninsula was separated from Ukraine by a border. Ukraine, supported by the international community, regards Crimea as temporarily occupied. In reaction to Russia's bordering activities, the Ukrainian state also had to build a border infrastructure along its side of the division line, including highly securitised exit-entry checkpoints (EECP).

In the following month, with the outbreak of military conflict in the southeastern industrial part of the Donbas (Ukraine's Donetsk and Luhansk *oblasts*) the Ukrainian government lost control over 400 km of its state border. After a phase of active hostilities with Russia-controlled military formations in the Donbas, the front line with the two quasi-state entities ('DPR' and 'LPR') was stabilised in the course of 2015. As a result of the Minsk II agreement, a new dividing contact line (a de facto border) and seven Ukrainian border checkpoints (EECP) were established along the line between Ukraine's government-controlled areas (UGCA) and the temporarily occupied territories. The two self-proclaimed republics cover a third of the Donbas territory. All Ukrainian state bodies and many other institutions (banks, universities, businesses) were relocated from Crimea and the Donbas temporarily occupied territories to other localities in Ukraine.

Current studies on borders and emerging bordering techniques (Amoor, Marmura, & Salter, 2008; Johnson et al., 2011; Paasi, 2011) stress that a border should no longer be viewed only as a fixed and fortified line with visible policing, but rather as a spatially and institutionally stretched system of practices and software systems (a 'virtual border'). After the annexation of Crimea and the onset of military conflict, the Ukrainian state had to establish both – it had to fortify its new military defence line (the contact line) and define border-crossing rules and procedures (conditions for crossing, permitted categories of population and goods, etc.). It also had to establish mechanisms of civil-military cooperation aimed at informing the population about military activities, assisting in the provision of humanitarian aid, coordinating infrastructure restoration, and de-mining activities (DCAF (Geneva Centre for Security Sector Governance), 2021). In a situation of military conflict, the government's defence and border securitisation measures unavoidably led to the appearance of both physical borders and symbolic ones, through the classification and labelling of its own citizens.

The state's power of nomination, certification, and accreditation is more often discussed in relation to contemporary migration governance – how passport systems, visa systems, and recognition of the migrants' educational and professional qualifications influence their status and facilitate/obstruct their integration. In the same way, this can be applied to the analysis of internal displacement when the state has to (re)admit its citizens and in many cases reissue legal and qualification documents. Regardless of the fact that IDPs moved within internationally recognised state boundaries and therefore were entitled to the full rights of other citizens, the emerging scholarship on legal violence (Menjívar & Abrego, 2012; Krasniqi & Stjepanović, 2015; Sardelić, 2015) demonstrates that state classification and certification procedures might produce 'uneven citizens' (Krasniqi & Stjepanović, 2015; Sardelić, 2015) in the internally displaced population. Ukrainian citizens who moved to the UGCAs had to prove their identity, and their belonging was questioned by numerous state identification procedures. Their freedom of movement was also limited as social workers had the right to visit the declared address of registration and check their presence; if absent, they could lose their status of IDP and its associated social benefits and rights. Moreover, their movement to and from the UGCAs was heavily regulated by a new system of border-crossing permits and registrations. Still, the intensity of contact line crossing prior to the pandemic was unprecedentedly high compared to similar protracted conflicts (on average 1.2–1.3 million crossings per month) (UNHCR, 2021).

The state was preoccupied with the securitisation of the border and defence measures were targeted primarily at ending the hot phase of the war; the population received less attention. Many IDPs in their interviews complain that the state was 'invisible' when they needed assistance with resettlement, but rather was imposing new barriers and limiting their rights. As a result, the populations of Crimea and the

Donbas were trapped in physical and symbolic boundary-producing practices, where the politics of identity and belonging now come into play.

Half a year after the annexation and beginning of the conflict over the Donbas, in October 2014, the Ukrainian government finally reacted to the resettlement problem and introduced the possibility of receiving IDP status.[25] The new laws initially aimed to give the IDPs some financial relief and strengthen guarantees to their rights and freedoms. In reality, it caused new troublesome bordering practices for those who applied. The identification, categorisation, and authorisation practices embedded in the law had a strong impact on the sense of belonging of the resettled populations. The new law provided a set of regulations on how the IDPs could use the rights and privileges associated with Ukrainian citizenship, and thus, in a sense, they had to prove their right to belong to the community.

The other problem was that in Ukraine access to practically all kinds of social benefits and other formal relationships with the state (private entrepreneur status, taxes, the banking system, health care, nurseries, the school system, and many others) are based on the still unreformed Soviet registration system (*propyska*). As a result, many IDPs, if not registered, did not have access to social benefits or to their private businesses (sometimes losing them completely). They were temporarily rendered immobile by the new identity verification and address registration procedures, having to prove every six months that they are domiciled at the same address. Furthermore, because their new permits did not count as long-term registration (*propyska*), they also lost their right to vote in local elections in their new place of residence. It took the Ukrainian state another seven years before it adopted its first 'Strategy for the Integration of Internally Displaced Persons',[26] which to a large degree was modelled on the 'European Union Action Plan on Integration of the Third-Country Nationals'. Its focus is mostly on providing affordable housing, access to education and the job market, access to basic social and health services, the replacement or recognition of identity cards and other formal documents, and only marginally touches upon issues of identity and integration to local communities. In this state policy, the strengthening of social cohesion and full

---

[25] Law of Ukraine, Verkhovna Rada of Ukraine, № 1706-VII: 'On ensuring rights and freedoms for internally displaced persons', 20.10.2014, available at: https://zakon.rada.gov.ua/laws/show/1706-18#Text, accessed 1 August 2021; after intensive advocacy campaigns between 2015 and 2021 the law was revised eleven times, after which many obstacles linked with the IDP status registration were resolved.

[26] Order of the Cabinet of Ministers of Ukraine, 2021 № 1364-r: Strategies for the integration of internally displaced persons and the implementation of medium-term solutions for internally displaced persons until 2024, 28 October 2021, available at: https://zakon.rada.gov.ua/laws/show/1364-2021-%D1%80?lang=en#Text, accessed 6 November 2021.

integration of the IDPs could be achieved through such superficial measures as the 'Development of standard provisions on advisory bodies for internally displaced persons' or the 'Development of methodical recommendations on the organisation of work of the centres of cultural services considering the needs of integration of internally displaced persons and the maintenance of their cultural rights and needs'.[27]

The analysis of the qualitative data demonstrates that resettlement from annexed or disputed territories to a new locality puts IDPs in the position of having to (re)negotiate their belonging to the community. The majority of IDPs who relocated to Ukrainian territories declared that on average they could not be easily differentiated from the locals, except in small rural or predominantly Ukrainian-speaking localities. Cultural and linguistic differences between the regions of Ukraine generally played a minimal role; it was rather, citizenship rights that became central to the self-understanding of the IDPs and their assertions of identity. The following quotations are some examples of how the IDPs framed and negotiated their belonging.

> We have such laws that if I do not register as a displaced person I am not counted as a resident of the country. I cannot open a business or bank account – this is outrageous! All of us moved here to assert our civic position and rights, and here we turned out to be non-citizens. It hurts (man, middle aged, resettled in Lviv from Bakhchisarai, 2016).

> I feel comfortable here. I have a right to live where I want. How can anybody say to me that I am not native or something similar? I am native! I live in Ukraine! (man, 35–54, from the Donbas, resettled in Dobropillia from Elenovka, 2016).

Respondents stressed that upon their resettlement the main group of people questioning their belonging were not local residents, but state officials. Their experience shows how state and street bureaucracies (Lipsky, 1980) dialogically produce IDPs out of ordinary citizens. The IDPs' borders of belonging were defined not so much by their experiences in the receiving communities, but mainly through the state's symbolic power of categorisation (laws, border regulations, recognition of documents, etc.), as well as in everyday interactions with low-level bureaucrats, whose discretionary decision-making shaped the IDPs multi-scalar incorporation (or exclusion) in the local community and the national body politic. Many of the IDPs interviewed said that the requirement to register, whereby the IDPs had to prove their right to belong to the community, affected their self-identity as Ukrainian citizens. IDPs often felt unjustly excluded and discriminated against or mistreated by state authorities (Bulakh,

---

[27] Ibidem, p. 7.

2020; Kuznetsova & Mikheieva, 2020; Sereda, 2020). Some IDPs deliberately distanced themselves from state structures and opted for 'contactless coexistence with the state' (up to one-third of the respondents did not register as displaced people) (Mikheieva & Sereda, 2015; Tronc & Nahikian, 2020) trusting instead civil society structures.

Numerous advocacy campaigns organised by the civil society activists in support of IDPs' rights gradually forced the Ukrainian government to acknowledge existing problems and improve bureaucratic or legislative limitations. When full-scale war broke in 2022, the Ukrainian government responded much quicker to the mass displacement. It also changed its approach to their registration. Since, compared to 2014, hostilities are taking place in a much larger territory of Ukraine, the government came up with a new tool – the e-governance portal 'Diya'. From March 13, citizens have the right to apply for a certificate and register their status as an internally displaced person. IDPs can also apply through 'Diya' for state financial assistance and other social benefits. In addition, the Portal allows instant access to various personal documents online and from any locality. This new digital governance tool allowed for uninterrupted service delivery even when millions were uprooted from their homes. However, this new procedure provoked dissatisfaction for some IDPs from the previous wave who accused government of preferential treatment of the new IDPs, and of creating new lines of inclusion and exclusion.

3.3 The Civil Society Response to Internal Displacement

3.3.1 Changing the Lens

I explore the involvement of IDP living in Ukraine, as well as of the receiving communities, through different forms of civic activism (formal or informal) and its role in giving the IDPs agency to rebuild their lives. According to the Guiding Principles on Internal Displacement accepted in 2005 on the basis of existing international humanitarian and human rights law, IDPs do not qualify as international refugees and, therefore, their own state is responsible for providing them with protection and aid (see the 'Responsibility to Protect' (R2P) concept). When the Ukrainian government, due to a lack of resources and experience, failed to produce adequate solutions, the state's failure became a major driver for the mobilisation of civil society in response to the IDP crisis. A certain paradox emerges from the literature, when, on the one hand, many studies report that civil society networks played an important role in the accommodation and integration of Ukrainian IDPs (UNDP, 2016; USAID, 2017; Worschech, 2017), on the other, Ukraine's civil society, like many other post-Soviet societies is often labelled as 'weak' (Foa & Ekiert, 2017).

In order to explain this, one needs to rethink the classical definition of 'civil society', which is outdated and rooted in Western European political thought. It is traditionally conceptualised as a sphere of active voluntary face-to-face civil associations and organisations that exist outside of the state, market, or family, and through which social cooperation and collective action take place (Howard, 2003; Way, 2014; Beissinger, 2017). Stewart stresses that 'To make the concept analytically useful and empirically manageable, many scholars have limited their analyses to formally registered non-governmental organisations' (Stewart & Dollbaum, 2017). Many international policy developing institutions adopted this approach. In fact, the United Nations Development Program (UNDP, 2016) describes civil society as non-governmental, non-state-related organisations that represent the interests of the members of public life. In the United States Agency for International Development (USAID's) report it is defined as a wide array of organisations – community groups, non-governmental organisations (NGOs), labour unions, indigenous groups, charitable organisations, faith-based organisations, professional associations, foundations, think tanks, and many others (USAID, 2017, p. 27). This approach is limited only to the institutionalised forms of civic engagement, measured through the number/ per cent of people belonging to NGOs or charitable foundations, or the number of registered organisations. Criticism of such an approach comes from several directions.

First, the analysis of civil society in post-communist countries has demonstrated that well-established NGOs are often elitist, disconnected from the public at large and could not fulfil their function of creating important nodal points that focus and lead social cooperation and collective action (Mendelson & Glenn, 2002; Lutsevych, 2013). Cooley and Ron (2002) find that inter-organisational competition for resources can lead humanitarian organisations towards 'dysfunctional outcomes'. All these critical points indicate a need for reconsidering the definitions of civil society and activism.

Following Dana Fisher's (2015) argument, I use a broader definition of civil activism, which includes broad forms of participation, defined as 'efforts by individuals as well as formal and informal collectives to affect social change'. Rather than focusing primarily on specific institutionalised actors, one should include non-formal actors and manifold ways of citizens' participation as different from more 'traditional' forms of activism, such as web activism (Earl & Kimport, 2011), urban activism (Aasland & Lyska, 2016), and seemingly everyday activities (Yukich, 2015) that bring social change, and, in this way, contribute to the strength of civil society empowering different social groups (in our case IDPs).

Social media and different internet platforms have become important drivers of civil society self-organisation. They serve as important channels of information exchange, sharply reduce costs for creating, organising, and participating, and decrease the need for activists to be physically together to act together (Earl & Kimport, 2011). Such informality allows a quick response, which is vital in a situation of unfolding humanitarian crises (like the one that is unfolding in Ukraine after Russia's invasion). It also creates a sense of openness and transparency between borders. It is especially important in the case of IDPs and the population living in the temporarily occupied territories of Crimea and the Donbas, where governmental and international aid organisations have limited access. Anyone can join informal networks at any time and for any period, without unnecessary formalities or obligations. One can even stay anonymous. The variety of forms and directions of interaction creates the possibility for simultaneous participation in various forms of social activism, taking into consideration the interests, needs, and resources of each person.

3.3.2 Receiving Communities' Response

The failure of the state to come up with a quick and adequate response prompted many established civil society organisations (CSOs) and volunteer groups active during the Euromaidan to restructure their profiles and regular activities. Moreover, Russia's annexation of Crimea and the military conflict over the Donbas stimulated an unprecedented wave of social mobilisation in support of the occupied territories. Macro-level analytical reports indicate that many new CSOs were established across the country to contribute to the aid effort and took over government responsibilities (USAID, 2017; DECAF, 2021; Tronc & Nahikian, 2020). Most of them emerged within the conflict zone, but also in the neighbouring regions that accommodated the largest number of IDPs. According to the DCAF study, between 2014 and 2017 the number of CSO members rapidly increased in the Donbas (twofold in Donetsk *oblast* and sixfold in Luhansk *oblast*).

Proliferation of CSOs formed to assist the relocated population is also indicative of deeper structural changes with Ukrainian civil society, first of all, by broadening the CSOs geography. Traditionally, their locations were limited to that of Ukraine's largest cities. Now they are moving, together with the displaced population, to all regions and all types of settlement. Secondly, these changes are reflected in the broadening and diversifying of the social groups involved. Finally, they are manifested in the differentiation of their activities. In the early stages of resettlement, the most common forms of aid provision were 'meeting the urgent material needs of IDPs, which include finding temporary accommodations and providing clothing, food, household items, medical attention, and information on registration. CSOs have also assisted IDPs in meeting their more long-term needs, including psychological support, employment assistance, social and legal services' (USAID, 2017). Step by step, IDP-related activism also became an important platform for the building of new trust networks projecting into the political and societal spheres (Worschech, 2017). This networking and cooperation among organisations took different forms: exchanging information and experiences, channelling suppliants' requests, partial engagement in other organisations' projects, implementing joint projects, obtaining organisational development services, participating in informal coalitions, and so on – although CSOs more often collaborated in advocacy campaigns as opposed to project implementation (Filipchuk, Lomonosova, & Slobodian, 2021).

A fundamental problem is that in analysing the role of civil society structures in IDP migration governance, researchers have focused primarily on registered CSOs and their networking and institutionalisation processes. However, the events of the past seven years in Ukraine have shown that such a formal – or in Bessinger's (2017) term 'conventional' – approach ignores other important types of social activism. The Euromaidan and later tragic events have spurred the emergence of numerous grassroots volunteer groups and informal networks providing support through both formal and informal channels (Burlyuk, Shapovalova, & Zarembo, 2017; Krasynska & Eric, 2017). Concentration on the formalised and easily measurable structures of civil society creates a rather distorted picture.

The DCAF's team, in their analysis of CSOs operating in the Donbas, found that, according to the Ministry of Justice of Ukraine, as of December 2020, there were over 5,000 CSOs registered in the Donetsk *oblast*, and more than 3,000 in Luhansk *oblast*. Of these, only 748 CSOs from the Donetsk *oblast* and 281 from the Luhansk *oblast* appeared to be active, and even fewer (382 for both *oblasts*) made available any detailed public information (DECAF, 2021, p. 2). This formal counting approach would lead us to conclude that civil society is non-functional. At the same time, in August 2019, according to the survey 'State of charitable practices in Ukraine' (Appendix 1 for detailed description), 65 per cent of the surveyed respondents from the Donetsk *oblast* declared that they had recently participated in charitable activities (mostly in the form of donating money or sharing food, clothes, and medicine). These numbers indicate how big the gap might be between everyday grassroots activism and statistically measurable formalised structures.

Such discrepancies could be explained by the fact that from the earliest stages of displacement, host communities were confronted with a need to respond quickly and flexibly – first to the short-term humanitarian needs of the arriving conflict-driven population (finding shelter, clothes, food and basic household items, access to social and medical services, legal or psychological assistance to traumatised individuals, etc.), and in the long run to assist their deeper integration. The over-bureaucratised formal CSOs could not react fast enough to the growing needs of IDPs. Where CSOs could not provide a quick enough response, grassroots activists and informal aid groups (or in many cases, ordinary citizens) stepped in.

The survey data allow us to analyse the regional specificity of declared civic engagement and the prevailing forms of participation in support of IDPs. In media discourse, the sides in the conflict are often described in ethnic terms – 'pro-Russian rebels' and 'pro-Ukrainian forces'. It is, therefore, important to investigate if there are any visible differences in the support of IDPs among respondents who self-identify as ethnic Ukrainians or ethnic Russians, or whose native language is Russian. This might disclose hidden patterns of inclusion/exclusion in the receiving communities.

Two consecutive surveys (Appendix 1 for their detailed description), conducted in March 2015 and November 2017, included questions about different types of activities practiced by the respondents during the previous year (for the full list of activities, see Appendix 2). Fifty-four per cent of the respondents in 2015 and 32 per cent in 2017 declared their involvement in at least one activity. The proposed list included a question about support for the IDPs. In 2015, 12.4 per cent of Ukrainians stated that they were assisting the IDPs from Crimea and the Donbas. This form of activism ranked third after 'assisting the army' (31 per cent), 'sharing resources' (money, food, etc.), and 'offering non-material assistance' (time, professional consultations, etc.)' which made up 18 per cent of the responses; the latter could also have included assistance to IDPs.

Map 7 shows the varying percentages of respondents in each *oblast* who chose the option 'assisting IDPs from Crimea and the Ukraine's East' in 2015 and 2017. It demonstrates that support for IDPs was not concentrated around those *oblasts* that hosted the highest percentage of officially registered IDPs, but was evenly distributed throughout the country. It also indicates that the level of involvement does not appear to be directly linked to the number of IDPs living in the region. The IDPs were unevenly settled in Ukraine. The highest numbers of IDPs are recorded in the regions close to the contact line. Their density gradually decreases towards the western and northern parts of the country. The western region, however, hosts the smallest percentage of the IDP population yet demonstrated the highest level of support.

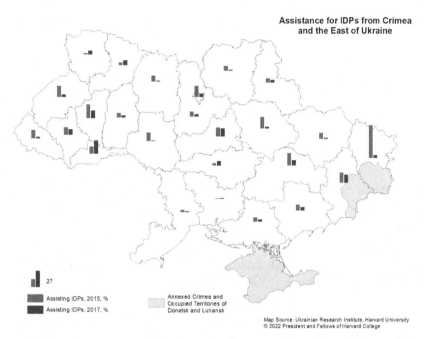

Map 7 Percentage of respondents who supported IDPs in 2015 and 2017[28]

Support of the IDPs had not only a broad geographical response, but also involved all strata of the population. A comparison of the respondents' socio-demographic characteristics did not show any significant differences between age and gender cohorts, income levels, size of locality or length of residence in the community, nationality or native language among those who supported the IDPs. This demonstrates how widespread and socially diverse the involvement was.

The survey 'State of Charitable Practices in Ukraine' shows that the civic engagement of Ukrainians had not dropped dramatically, even by 2021, but had changed its orientation. When in August 2019 respondents were asked whether during the previous twelve months they had been personally involved in charitable activity, helping someone or volunteering, 60 per cent answered positively. In August 2021 this number increased to 67 per cent. Among the most popular forms of engagement were: 'donated money' (88 per cent), 'shared food, clothes, medicine' (41 per cent), and 'offered free services to the community' (9 per cent). This suggests that two-thirds of Ukraine's

---

[28] *Map Source*: Harvard Ukrainian Research Institute (HURI) open online project, available at: https://gis.huri.harvard.edu/donbas-and-crimea-focus; *Data Source*: Survey 'Region, Nation, and Beyond: An Interdisciplinary and Transcultural Reconsideration of Ukraine' conducted in March 2015 and 15 October–1 November 2017.

population was in some way involved in informal aid networks. The sharing of material goods was more common in big cities (51 per cent), where the displaced population is mostly concentrated. Still, only 4 per cent of the respondents claimed that they were helping IDPs directly (16 per cent in the Donetsk *oblast*, and 9 per cent in the Luhansk *oblast*).

Among those who donated money, 65 per cent gave directly to the recipients and 21 per cent deposited money directly into bank accounts. This testifies that the largest amount of all donations was made directly to those in need within the communities, and therefore went unnoticed in studies focusing on formal institutions. Such behaviour might be explained by the necessity for a quick response to the urgent needs of IDPs, or by fears that the modest resources respondents are able to share will shrink even further after the deduction of fees for intermediary transactions.

These quantitative data show that the civil society structures (both formal and informal) attempted to compensate for the failures of the government. The IDPs, in their interviews, describe a wide variety of aid practices offered by the host communities, most of which are in the sphere of informal interactions. Among these are providing free accommodation; raising funds; sharing food, clothes, and medicine; offering jobs; offering free legal, medical, or psychological consultations; offering language or skill training; excursions and many more.

3.3.3 IDP Engagement

It is important to stress that the response of civil society should not be viewed one-sidedly, narrowly confined to humanitarian undertakings by the host communities, and the IDPs should not be seen exclusively as passive recipients of this assistance. From the earliest stages of displacement, a whole range of IDP self-help groups were established that soon formed bigger networks. The 'Crimea-SOS' after Russia's annexation of the peninsula and several more SOS-type organisations were founded after the beginning of the war in the Donbas. They combined a broad spectrum of activities centred on helping the conflict-affected population on both sides of the contact line. Later, wider collaborative platforms were established that led to the advocacy movement for both the IDPs and the population of the temporarily occupied territories of Ukraine, helping to correct the many oversights in state IDP migration governance policies. Some of those collaborative platforms also became the UNHCR's presence and coverage partners. However, the real level of IDP engagement is difficult to estimate because of the wide diversity of funding institutions and initiatives (international, national, and local) and the relatively high proportion of informal self-aid activism.

It should also be stressed that many studies wrongly portray Ukrainian IDPs as a single group (UNDP, 2016; USAID, 2017; Mudde, 2018). In reality, as discussed earlier, decisions to stay or leave Crimea and the Donbas were based on very different circumstances. What is more, the IDP population represents different political, age, social, ethnic and cultural groups, including the Muslim population of Crimea. The analysis of interviews with the resettled population revealed that there was one group, the Crimean Tatars, whose strategies of engagement differed from other IDPs coming from both Crimea and the Donbas. This phenomenon could be explained by the fact that Crimean Tatars had a recent experience of deportation (by the Stalin regime in 1944) and repatriation after the dissolution of the Soviet Union. Thus, they resorted to strategies of survival acquired during their deportation to Central Asia and later return to their Crimean homeland after 1991. Furthermore, in many cases, those who left Crimea were activists, who had fled fearing persecution. Immediately upon resettlement, the Crimean Tatar IDPs adopted strategies of active cooperation with the government and local administrations (in terms of acquiring IDP registration, renewing or applying for licenses for private entrepreneurship, appealing for land plots, etc.), even when they had to deal with an absence of procedures, gaps in legislation, and negative attitudes on the part of low-level bureaucrats. Among their most important group-empowerment strategies were, firstly, the establishment of their own businesses (in particular, ethnic and fast-food restaurants) which helped, partially, to solve their unemployment problem, and secondly, the development of their human capital by sending Crimean Tatar youth to universities (especially in the EU).

> We can't go around begging for something. Our country is in such a state now that it's not we who should be asking for something, but it's our country that is in need, so we should help in any way we can: by giving bread, providing a kind word or a prayer. Such are the times we live in (man, old, Crimean Tatar resettled to Lviv from Crimea, 2014).

> We should send our youth abroad, so they will get the best European education possible. And then, one day, when Crimea will be free, they will know how to rebuild it (man, middle-aged, Crimean Tatar resettled to Warsaw from Crimea, 2016).

Right from the early stages of their relocation, the Crimean Tatars actively cooperated with local volunteer organisations and relied on their help, but they often initiated CSOs or voluntary networks themselves. The IDPs from the Donbas adopted a different tactic. In the early stages of their resettlement, many tried to avoid direct contact with the government. Among their expressed concerns were relatives or property left behind in the temporarily occupied territories, or the fear of being drafted into the Ukrainian army fighting a war over the Donbas. At this stage, they had to rely more on aid offered by volunteer organisations and local informal networks, in which they also actively participated themselves. For many IDPs from Crimea and the Donbas, another important form of activism, besides establishing self-support networks, became the support of Ukrainian army units fighting for the Donbas. They often described this form of activism as their patriotic duty, reinforcing their civic sense of belonging.

The intensive influx of a new population brought developmental and infrastructural challenges to many Ukrainian cities, especially those in the East, which hosted the biggest share of the relocated population. A strong impact on social change was made by the IDPs who can be described as highly qualified professionals, predominantly from the major cities like Donetsk or Luhansk. In their home cities they were accustomed to a much wider spectrum of social services and leisure activities, including extracurricular education, children's afterschool programmes and sports, which were lacking in their new receiving communities. Their solution was to recreate the missing services themselves. Those who knew foreign languages or had experience of working with international donor organisations served as mediators in directing humanitarian aid or implementing social and infrastructural changes. As a result, relocation generated a powerful wave of urban activism aimed at assisting the IDPs' adaptation and overcoming of new infrastructural challenges. Many young and middle-aged respondents confessed that resettlement had a positive effect on their lives by liberating them from everyday routines and enabling them to change their jobs, learn new skills, start a new business, move to a better location, or become civically engaged. In interviews one can find accounts of changes brought about by the IDPs' cooperation with the local administration and urban activists. Many displaced people, in their interviews, stressed that they had difficulties finding jobs in almost all locations, but especially in small towns dominated by a single industry and located close to the contact line which hosted a large portion of the IDP population fleeing the Donbas. This situation pushed many of them to search for new solutions through different start-up initiatives or by launching new businesses.

Furthermore, IDPs, in cooperation with local activists, played an active role in the 'rebranding' of the Eastern region by helping to shape new identities for post-Soviet industrial cities of the region, and for the local communities to discover a new sense of belonging. The decommunisation process launched in the country by the Euromaidan protests created space for the (re)discovery of pre-Soviet heritage and initiated an active movement in 'search of their roots', and a boom in local history discussions and initiatives. The UGCA of the

Donbas, as well as other Eastern and Southern Ukrainian industrial cities, became centres of transformation of local symbolic landscapes. In their search for new possibilities, many Ukrainian cities started to reproduce European practices of revitalising historical and industrial heritage sites and turning them into tourist attractions. Such initiatives required the 'invention' of new city identities that would be attractive to both Ukrainian and foreign tourists. For many Donbas cities it also entailed a detachment from the stigma of war. IDPs, in cooperation with scholars and local activists, used the presence and financial assistance of Western foundations for active involvement in the Donbas rebranding (e.g., the project 'Donkult' in Lviv and Kyiv, and various touristic forums).[29] Involvement in processes of gentrification, and the possibility to help host communities to redefine their status and 'identities' within the nation, advanced the IDPs' integration.

The wide spectrum of IDPs' activities aimed at social change such as urban activism, sharing information and resources, building up common services not only empowered them, but helped to negotiate their new place within the receiving communities which benefited from new services and businesses that developed with the help of the dislocated populations. This integration strategy helped upgrade the quality of life and diversify job markets in the receiving communities. At the same time, IDPs stress that involvement in self-aid networks and different forms of activism gave them an empowering feeling of being 'useful' or of 'giving' and, thus, of being legitimate members of the local communities. It stimulated an undercurrent of transformative change occurring inside Ukrainian society, making it more resilient and creating a new sense of belonging not through origin, regional or religious affiliation, ethnicity or culture, but by doing something together or helping each other to overcome difficulties.

The full-scale Russian war produced an unprecedented wave of in-country and cross-border displacement happening within a noticeably brief period. This crisis became a new test of the resilience and mobilisation capacities – first of the Ukrainian society, and soon of its neighbours, especially Poland and Moldova, who were the first to accept thousands of Ukrainian refugees daily during March and April. Within a short period of time, self-aid networks and volunteer groups were established at all levels throughout the country. In May 2022 (InfoSapience, 2022) 65 per cent of surveyed Ukrainians admitted

---

[29] Tourist potential of the Donetsk and Luhansk *oblasts* presented at international summit in Kyiv, *Biznes-Sxid*, 3 October 2019, available at: https://bizshid.com/news/1521-turystychnu-donechchynu-i-luhanshchynu-predstavliaiut-na-mizhnarodnomu-samiti-u-kyievi, accessed 11 May 2021; Project 'Donkult', available at: https://city-adm.lviv.ua/news/culture/225403-vzhe-nezabarom-u-lvovi-startuie-kulturnyi-forum-donkult, accessed 11 May 2021.

that they were helping IDPs (32 per cent were sharing food, 20 per cent volunteered and another 20 per cent donated money, 14 per cent provided accommodation). Moreover, a quarter of the displaced admitted helping other IDPs. According to the UNHCR (2022) report the number of IDPs in Ukraine is about 7 million. At the same time, the Ministry of Social Policy reported slightly over 2.7 million people who had registered for and received IDP certificates by early May.[30] This statistic shows that almost two-thirds of the displaced rely on their own resources or on the support of the civil society.

The practices of self-organisation, described earlier, and the various forms of activism aimed at supporting the displaced in Ukraine could become a starting point for future enquiries studying the response of the population of neighbouring countries to the arrival of millions of Ukrainians. Moreover, fleeing cross-border Ukrainians continued to demonstrate elevated levels of solidarity and self-organisation. They were reproducing learned patterns of self-organisation by creating social media self-aid networks and volunteer groups that provide various forms of assistance in their new receiving communities. Many support networks were utilising existing diaspora structures of cross-border cooperation initiatives and academic exchange networks. The active cooperation of displaced Ukrainians with local civil society activists and volunteers facilitated the process of adaptation and isolation, strengthening the lines of solidarity with the population in receiving countries. A survey conducted in April 2022 among the Ukrainian refugees in Poland, Germany, and Ireland demonstrated that at this early stage of resettlement, respondents already knew several people from Ukrainian groups and several from the local population, whom they could address if they had some problems (Isański et al., 2022).

However, this new crisis illustrated that internationally recognised displacement policies need to be reconsidered. Previous models presupposed that the primary responsibility for providing early response and humanitarian aid would fall first and foremost on the state (in the case of internal displacement), on host states and on the big international organisations (in the case of transborder refugee migration). The analysis of the early stage of Ukrainian cross-border displacement shows that local government and state structures lagged behind civil society responses and actively stepped in only after some period of time. Similarly, long-standing international organisations like the International Red Cross, Human Rights Watch, and others, founded by idealists and ground-breaking in their time, have now often turned into clumsy over-bureaucratised corporations incapable of quick and flexible responses. New models of displacement governance should take into consideration that the

---

[30] Ministry of Social Policy. (2022). *5,2 mil'yarda hryven' pererakhovano dlya vyplaty dopomohy na prozhyvannya vnutrishn'o peremishchenym osobam*, 6 May, available at: www.msp.gov.ua/news/21804.html, accessed 30 September 2022.

new forms of self-organisation and volunteering could better facilitate fast responses to an evolving crisis.

4 Testing the Boundaries of Inclusion and Exclusion: IDPs' Connections and Disconnections with Social Groups, Places, and Trends of Memory (Re)production

In this section I analyse how war (re)shapes narratives of belonging and mnemonic practices of local communities in Ukraine and the nature of the role of IDP in these processes. In the last section, following Vanessa May's concept of belonging (May, 2013), I explore the multidimensional and complex connections and disconnections that displaced people experience with regard to the historical past, their new places of residence, and the social groups that they perceive as important. Since the military conflict reinforces different cultural markers of belonging, and IDPs represent different ethnic and cultural groups, including the Muslim population of Crimea, this requires the application of a transcultural approach. An in-depth analysis of the IDPs and receiving communities shall uncover how local memories interact with prevalent meta-narratives and how they are influenced by the transnational trends of memory production and reproduction

4.1 Hierarchies of Group Belonging

I will explore the multidimensional and complex connections and disconnections that IDPs experience in relation to their past, their new places of residence, and the social groups that they perceive as important. I examine whether relocation from the same territory (e.g., Crimean Tatars and non-Crimean Tatars coming from Crimea), relocation to the same territory, or belonging to the same ethno-linguistic group, could be decisive in defining how a sense of belonging is experienced in everyday interactions by the Ukrainian IDPs and what social groups and identity markers become most salient for them. I also focus on what impact the (re)shaped mnemonic landscapes and practices of receiving communities in Ukraine had on the IDPs and what the role of the IDP might be in these processes.

4.1.1 The Internally Displaced Population in Government-Controlled Territories

When asked who they see as responsible for the conflict, respondents constantly describe it as imported and nurtured from above – from the Kremlin/Russia or from Kyiv/Washington/Brussels, but not from within their region. Moreover, the conflict in the Donbas is almost never described as ethnic, but as political/civilisational or, less often, as a fight for resources.

When respondents describe their life before the conflict they do not talk about ethnic or linguistic conflicts in the Donbas before 2014. If asked directly, they stress that cultural-linguistic differences were of no importance in their region and in the neighbouring regions of Ukraine. They explain it using the Soviet policies of labour migration that often forced people to move and mix. In Crimea, respondents of Ukrainian and Russian origin use the same narrative of a peaceful coexistence between different ethnic groups. They describe national identity as insignificant for them and for the other inhabitants of the region. Respondents from both regions believed that attempts to articulate national differences were imposed politically, from above, and describe them as the result of manipulation. It could also be argued that in the case of the Donbas no visible ethnic conflicts were registered prior to the Euromaidan, and earlier studies also point to the lesser significance of ethnic/national identities in the region (Ryabchuk, 2003; Sereda, 2006). In her study, Maria Lewicka (2007) showed that the inhabitants of those *oblasts* more frequently choose their own place and region, as well as Eastern Europe as their main object of self-identification as opposed to nation-related categories. At the same time, this declared attachment to the place of residence (neighbourhood, town/village) and local neighbourly ties was weaker than among the inhabitants of the western *oblasts* of Ukraine. In the case of Crimea, this narrative of the conflict-less coexistence of different ethnic groups can be viewed as a reproduction of the innate Soviet propaganda promoting the 'friendship of all nations', which allowed existing ethno-cultural inequalities to be covered over. Interviews with Crimean Tatar respondents pointed to numerous cases of discrimination against their group and conflicts happening from the beginning of their repatriation in the 1990s which were simply ignored by local and central government.

IDPs admitted that they were going through a very intensive process of understanding their belonging which involved different levels of their previous group affiliations. To some extent, their broader social identity was threatened by local authorities in Ukraine, Russia, Poland, or any other country of their relocation and by the need to (re)assert and prove their right to belong there. Moreover, respondents stressed that they did not want to be associated with a broad category of 'IDPs' or 'refugees', because this label is, in their view, a source of hierarchisation and othering that often portrays them as a powerless and victimised group or as people who are viewed with suspicion because they might themselves (or their relatives, who stayed behind the contact line) support separatists. Some also reported mutual stereotyping when those IDPs who came from Crimea, and in some cases IDPs from the Donbas, tried to differentiate themselves from others arriving from the Donbas claiming that they are pro-separatists or have an 'old Soviet and paternalistic worldview'.

Many admitted that the conflict, displacement, and their everyday interactions in the new receiving communities created situations where they felt strongly that they had lost their sense of belonging both to the regional Donetsk (and to a lesser extent Crimean) community and to their local community of neighbours and family. They reported feeling pushed to redefine their belonging to the wider imagined communities – be it transnational (sometimes imagined previously as Slavic, East Slavic, or Soviet) or national (Ukrainian, Russian). IDPs often reported alienation from their own local community or from relatives and family members, especially at the early stages of resettlement because of the difference in their views. At the same time, their new social ties within the receiving community developed slowly and would not yet allow them to generate a strong feeling of belonging. The choice of words in their interviews testifies to the fact that in their narratives those who resettled try to avoid precise categorisations and describe their new situation using the widest possible groupings. Interview word counts show that they use the categories 'we/us', and 'people/humans' ten times more than 'locals', 'compatriots', 'Ukrainians or Russians', or 'IDPs'. However, IDPs involved in formal or informal activist networks reported much less disorientation or sense of being lost.

Interviews show that IDPs are using different tactics to build their sense of belonging to the receiving communities, often based on identities prevailing in their regions or groups before the conflict. Those who moved from the Donbas build their sense of belonging through stressing their urban, social, or professional identities, creating a differentiation with smaller localities or the countryside and an identification with an all-Ukrainian urban space, not with Russian-speaking or regional spaces (the category 'city' is used in their interviews over twenty times more often than 'countryside' or 'district', and three times more often than 'country' or 'Donbas'). At the same time, IDPs from the Donbas, in their narratives of belonging, display a weak attachment to regional identity. Those who have moved to Ukrainian-controlled areas of the Donbas do not demonstrate a higher level of attachment to those localities than IDPs who have moved to other Ukrainian cities or towns. Only a small number of respondents describe themselves as 'Donetskites' or 'inhabitants of the Donbas'. For them, a more distinguishing marker is belonging to 'urban civilisation', and sometimes to the Soviet ethos of mining, which was cultivated in family histories.

Those who moved from Crimea (but not Crimean Tatars) stress their regional identity – Crimean. Crimean Tatars stress their ethno-linguistic, regional, and for those who are religious, Muslim identities. For them, attachment to the region and local symbolic landscapes is a key element of their narrative of belonging. In the narratives of the Crimean Tatar IDPs, locality and ethnicity form the core through which their belonging is structured. In their interviews, they present a structured complex historical narrative with detailed descriptions of Crimean Tatar locality as well as symbolic spaces on the Black Sea and Crimean Tatar historical events. An urban-rural division is not so important for them. Partially, this can be explained by their previous experience of repatriation, when many Crimean Tatars were denied the possibility of settling in cities but were given land-plots in the Crimean steppe. Therefore, although Crimean Tatars moved to large urban centres (Kyiv, Lviv, and Kherson), their strategy was to ask local governments to provide their community with plots of land for small housing projects in the surrounding countryside.

The utilisation of different markers of belonging by the IDPs from the Donbas and Crimean Tatars are most visible when one analyses events or activities aimed at public outreach within their receiving communities. Beginning from the early stages of relocation, Crimean Tatar communities stressed their ethnic, cultural, and religious differences. For this purpose, they organised into formal or informal national-cultural centres. They would use different means (commemorations, workshops, theatrical performances, social media portals, etc.) to promote Crimean Tatar culture and heritage.

The IDPs from the Donbas used different tactics. They organised events aimed at the de-stigmatisation of the IDP community emphasising the message that 'we are like you'. They would contest the narratives labelling them as 'separatists' and complaining that the pro-Ukrainian or pro-Euromaidan resistance in the Donbas was being overlooked. Another important strategy is the creation of online collections of oral testimonies, virtual museums, exhibitions, and social media portals.[31] They were also involved in the rebranding and 're-imagining' of the Donbas as well as of other Eastern Ukrainian industrial cities.

Forced displacement triggers anxieties and concerns that lie at the heart of national identity: questions arise of who can belong to a national community and on what grounds. In Ukraine this new dynamic was created by the displacement when both sides – resettled people and receiving communities – were forced to rethink the terms of their belonging to the national community. Shifts in national self-understanding of Ukrainian society were described earlier.

Practically, all those interviewed claim to be bi- or trilingual (both Russian- and Ukrainian-speaking or Russian-, Ukrainian- and a minority language-speaking) but admit that normally they use only Russian in their everyday communication, so the displacement (mostly to the nearest big industrial cities

---

[31] Museum of Civilian Voices founded by the Rinat Akhmetov Foundation https://akhmetovfounda tion.org/en/rinat-ahmetov-dopomozhemo/project/golosy-myrnyh-muzey-fondu-rinata-ahmetova? fbclid=IwAR0cL99ubOH3weOb5VoaiT33z7XwD3bGB1nl8TGYbbDut9iPKuwoGgkM C20, Project 'Heroes of Ukrainian Donbas' funded by the Ministry of Culture and Information Policy https://youtu.be/rLkA5sGwTyU, https://youtu.be/fr1RaQMEc18.

often predominantly Russian-speaking) has not radically changed their linguistic practices. Only a tiny minority claimed that they changed their language of everyday communication to Ukrainian either in protest against Russia's aggression, to demonstrate their loyalty as a citizen or because they found themselves in a predominantly Ukrainian-speaking environment.

When the interviewees described their sense of national belonging, the prevailing differentiation was between an ethnocultural sense of *nationality*, transmitted through the family origin, and according to the Soviet concept and practice of 'natsionalnost' is their 'ascribed nationality' and the political sense of citizenship. Later, this was often described as the most important form of self-identity, based on individual experience:

> I just know my family history. For hundreds of years back they all were ethnic Russians. By blood I am Russian, but by my feelings – I am a Ukrainian nationalist (man, young, resettled from Sevastopol to Kharkiv, 2014).

Many (especially those who moved from the Donbas) admitted that in the past, national identity was of lesser importance to them, but when the conflict erupted and their national belonging was questioned, they felt strong bonds with their 'Ukrainianness' (based on such markers as citizenship, national symbols, cultural traditions, experience of fighting for democracy, etc.). Those who defined themselves as Russians described their identity mostly through the concept of 'ascribed nationality' (by ethnicity of parents). Rarely was it described as a preference for language ('I think in Russian') or high culture ('I read Russian literature'). Often it was described as either unimportant ('Just the name and no special pride in that', 'just a line in my passport') or as not being mutually exclusive with also being Ukrainian:

> Ukraine is my homeland, but my native language is Russian. I was born here and I speak this language. I know Ukrainian very well, but if you think in Russian, then why lie and say I'm Ukrainian? (woman, middle-aged, resettled from Luhansk to Kharkiv, 2014).

> Ethnically Russian because I have all my roots in the Rostov region. By nationality – Ukrainian. By citizenship and self-understanding – Ukrainian (man, young, resettled from Sinzhne to Kyiv, 2017).

4.1.2 The Population Living in the Temporarily Occupied Territories

In this context, it is also interesting to compare how respondents who live in the temporarily occupied territories of the Donbas articulate their identities. Interviews demonstrate an absence of exclusivist Russian nationalistic narratives both among the military and civilian population. In their narratives of belonging, the anti-government separatists who joined military units often used vague transnational Slavic or Soviet descriptions of identity, with Russian/ Ukrainian ethnicity subordinated:

> Nationality – Slav. There is such a nationality as Slav. I am Russian Slav (man, young, TOT of the Donbas, 2016).

> Slavic. I do not divide between Russian, Ukrainian, Belarusian. I am a Slav. I feel that way. I was recorded as Ukrainian. For me Slav means unity with my brothers in blood, in spirit. It is a way of thinking and living, with those who live in the territory sharing our religion (man, middle-aged, temporarily occupied territories of the Donbas, 2016).

The civilian population demonstrates a strong Donbas regional identity and connectedness to the region ('I was born here I will die here'). In national terms, a minority self-identified as Russians and the majority as Ukrainians. However, both groups use same formulas of ascribed nationality and a harmonious coexistence of two ethnicities. They often defined their belonging to a group through cultural preferences:

> Mixed marriage: Russian mother, Ukrainian father and the family had full respect for both nationalities. We had Ukrainian songs. Well, it was a model of absolute calm and harmonious existence (woman, old, Donetsk, 2016).

> Russian. It's not written in the passport now. Russian as my mother (woman, middle-aged, Yasinovataia, 2016).

> I was born in the territory of the former Soviet Union, even if in Ukraine. Still, the Russian language, Russian traditions and Russian people are closer to us (woman, middle-aged, Crimea, 2016).

> I feel like a turncoat going back and forth. Russian? Who knows? I speak two languages, I am a bit Russian, but actually I am Ukrainian. I have lived in Ukraine all my life, so I am Ukrainian. I am Russian because I studied in a Russian school, but my Motherland is Ukraine (woman, old, Stakhanov, 2016).

When the Ukrainian identity is stressed, the important markers of belonging are language and traditions, not used in everyday life but used by relatives, and are therefore used in the description of being native. For the younger generation another important factor is territorial or citizenship affiliation. They feel Ukrainian because they were born in Ukraine or because the Donbas is Ukrainian territory:

> *I'm simply Ukrainian. My Donbas is dear to me and the fact that it is in Ukraine makes me believe that I am Ukrainian* (woman, middle aged, Donetsk, 2016).

Many respondents admit that they were nationally indifferent, but war and an absence of Ukrainian symbols made them realise their Ukrainianness:

> It was only with the war that I realised that I am connected to Ukraine, that I want to be in Ukraine, and I am a pro-Ukrainian citizen. It was being in the 'DPR,' being in the war that made me realise it (woman, middle-aged, Donetsk, 2016).

What one can observe here contradicts the stereotypical description of the population that lives in the temporarily occupied territories as pro-Russian separatists. The majority of them have a mixed identification where Russian and Ukrainian identities are strongly intertwined and not mutually exclusive. However, this situation is not stable. The protracted conflict, restrictive regime of the self-proclaimed states, and limited contact with the outside may gradually shift the balance of the inhabitants' national loyalties and sense of belonging (Sasse & Lackner, 2018). However, a sense of belonging has two other important dimensions – those that are temporal and spatial.

4.2 Spatial Dimensions of Belonging

During resettlement the displaced population goes through the process of de-territorialisation (detachment from their immediate localities) and re-territorialisation to the new receiving localities. It triggers the refiguration of their understanding of, and attachment to, space and markers of place. As a consequence of the military conflict, or annexation, for many interviewed, a surrounding space previously imagined as boundless or trans-local (such as the Slavic world or the Russian-Ukrainian borderland) suddenly became, as a consequence of military conflict or annexation, a forced emplacement with strictly controlled borders. Similarly, as a result of the war and the ensuing displacement, many started to pay more attention to cultural or historical symbolic markers, such as flags, monuments, and religious buildings present in the surrounding space, which had previously been 'invisible' in their every-day interactions. These then began to play an important role in the sense of belonging or, alternately, generated a feeling of detachment: 'I do not belong here because I am surrounded by foreign symbols, architecture, environment'.

For many, displacement created a strong sense of a lost home or place when the comfortable and peaceful local space suddenly became dangerous and the focus of a violent national and international struggle. When asked how they see their region's future, the majority opted for a defined legal space: 'when all laws are working' whether Ukrainian or Russian, but not with the status of an unrecognised territory or buffer zone between Ukraine and Russia. In interviews conducted after 2017, many admitted that they first believed that the Donbas would be fully integrated into Russia, but after some time they reconsidered their views. They expressed the wish that it would soon be reintegrated into Ukraine.

Interviewees do not conform to the stereotypical assumption that those of Russian origin would support the idea that temporarily occupied territories should go to Russia rather than Ukraine – supporting, more often, the idea that they should go to Ukraine. Many respondents, who claim to be of Russian origin, explicitly articulated their wish for the Donbas or Crimea to return to Ukrainian control and exist under Ukrainian borders, remaining as they were before the conflict. Besides the customary argument that these were Ukrainian territories by law and that the post-war order should not be altered, many explain that, in comparison, the Ukrainian state gives their citizens more freedom and democracy.

The mechanism of nostalgia for a lost place differs in the narrative of all groups of displaced people. For the IDPs from the Donbas the local space they came from is often narrated and defined, not by a particular locality (be it the metropolis of Donetsk or a small town), but rather by the immediate spaces of everyday interaction (such as the home, the shop, the place of work, the school, or the hospital), and sometimes by particular streets. In their narratives 'house' or 'apartment' are the most frequently used categories. IDPs from the Donbas often show a lack of articulated interest in the local history of their own city or region. The remembered space is more often marked through non-historical local markers such as the garden of forged sculptures or the Donbas Arena or social groups such as family, friends, neighbours, and colleagues. Alienation from the locality is often described as alienation from the people:

> I am offended when they say those things about the Donbas. Those, who were able, they left. Those who stayed, besides pensioners who simply did not have other possibilities or those who could pay rents there but have housing here; others who stayed . . . they have a very primitive level. They have no culture at all! When I was there, I just wanted to go through it like a tunnel as quickly as possible and not touch any of these people (woman, middle aged, resettled from Luhansk *oblast* to Basel, 2021).

A large number of respondents claimed that even if their region were to be reintegrated it would no longer be 'their' place, because people who now live there make it foreign to them. They expressed their wish to stay in their new places of residence.

The most remembered symbolic markers of local space are monuments belonging to the Soviet or Soviet Ukrainian metanarratives – Lenin, Shevchenko, or Second World War memorials. However, this Soviet historical nostalgia does not contradict their Ukrainian political patriotism. Interest in the local past, architecture, cultural, and historical heritage was triggered in the process of re-territorialisation and is pronounced in relation to the new places of residence. The need to become familiar with new urban spaces frequently provoked interest in the new memoryscapes.

IDPs from both regions often stress that initially they felt lost in their new receiving localities:

> When you grow up in one place, you absorb something at the level of traditions, culture, you still understand that this is a church, there is a school ... It shapes you somehow. You are the carrier of this information. And when you come here, it is a complete black hole! (woman, old, resettled from Avdiivka to Warsaw, 2016).

Depending on the region of resettlement, the feeling of a general loss of familiar urban and social space could also resonate with the lack of knowledge about the symbolic markers present in their new communities. The comparison of regions with the most intensive decommunisation landscape shifts with the regions hosting the highest number of officially registered IDPs in Ukraine (Map 8)

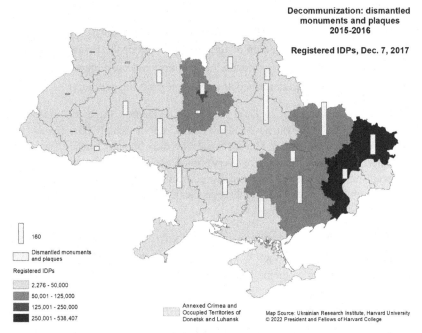

Map 8 Comparison of regions hosting the highest number of officially registered IDPs (2017) with the number of demolished monuments in the process of decommunisation in 2015–2016[32]

---

[32] *Map Source*: Harvard Ukrainian Research Institute (HURI) open online project, available at: https://gis.huri.harvard.edu/donbas-and-crimea-focus; *Data Source*: data provided by the UNHCR and the Ukrainian Institute of National Memory.

suggests that the displaced population found itself in the localities that were at the epicentre of recodification battles caused by the decommunisation. Simultaneously, due to the close proximity of those locations to the conflict zone, their cityscapes were heavily filled with new mnemonic spaces devoted to the new cult of heroes.

Those decommunisation and symbolic recodification processes coincided with the IDPs' attempts to explore and accommodate themselves in their new localities. Many interviewees admitted that these processes affected their search for belonging in their new communities. Some respondents admitted that decommunisation at the place of their resettlement pushed them to rethink their attitudes towards the Soviet and Russian imperial past and specifically about the persons commemorated by the toppled monuments or new toponyms. On the other hand, many IDPs expressed their disapproval of the decommunisation policy because it amplified their feeling of being lost or strengthened their detachment. Valeria Lazarenko (2021, p. 9) in her study of the reclaiming of urban spaces by the IDPs demonstrated that for some, the renaming of their native towns made them feel and talk about their hometowns 'as a distant, almost unreachable, and even ghost-like place – as their town (the way they remember it) does not exist on a map anymore'. For many, decommunisation created a situation where one place is symbolically absent or has negative connotations (as a war/occupation zone) and the new place is unknown and uncharted. This strongly influenced feelings of belonging. Some respondents complained that decommunisation coupled with the process of an intensive symbolic marking of cities as Ukrainian[33] (by flags or national colours), made them feel under pressure and pushed them back to the temporarily occupied territories. For others, Ukrainian symbols became a very important part of their sense of belonging to a community or to the Ukrainian nation ('As soon as I see Ukrainian flag, I know I am home'). An important finding for the governance of migration is the significance of building social ties by walking through a city, learning about its historical heritage, visiting museums, or going on excursions, and that these may become vital practices in helping IDPs or refugees overcome their re-territorialisation difficulties and develop a strong sense of belonging to a new locality. In their research, Maria Lewicka and Bartłomiej Iwańczak (2019) demonstrated that attachment to a new place of residence and the interest taken in its history have a positive correlation with group identifications (regional, national) dominant, or at least highly respected, in the region. My research confirms her findings. Familiarity with space and its symbolic markers

---

[33] A process actively happening in 2015 as a reaction to Russian propaganda and the possibility of further separatist uprisings in the so-called 'Novorossia' when many industrial cities in the east and south were marked with Ukrainian colours and symbols by the city dwellers.

allowed respondents not only to feel included in the urban environment, but to also strengthen their sense of belonging to the local or national community by learning more about them and their past. In relation to these experiences, IDPs or those who moved abroad admitted that intensive exploration of the city and learning about its history or current affairs helped them to feel like real residents of the city, allowing them to finally describe themselves as 'Kharkivites', or a 'Kherson resident'. Moreover, Lewicka (2013) demonstrated that active attachment to a place (a place discovered through an active effort in order to appropriate it) is strongly linked to the person's experience of agency. Therefore, active efforts to discover their new place of residence also help displaced people to strengthen their agency.

In February 2022, after the beginning of the full-scale Russian aggression, many cities in Ukraine and in neighbouring countries experienced a massive new wave of both decommunisation (linked to the revision of the Soviet cult of the Great Patriotic war) and/or de-Russification of public places and memoryscapes. On the contrary, however, monuments of Lenin were reinstalled and Soviet flags were hoisted on administrative buildings in those cities that were occupied by Russia.

4.3 Temporal Dimensions of Belonging

Besides a feeling of spatial dislocation, for many of those interviewed, displacement created a strong sense of interrupted time ('before' the events of 2014, and 'after'). In the IDPs' interviews, the Euromaidan is often a starting point around which they structure their narratives about events that took place in their regions (Crimea or the Donbas). Regardless of their position, for many of them, Euromaidan serves as a marker of the rupture of normal temporality and the beginning of radical change, which subsequently led to their forced relocation. In some cases, Euromaidan is strongly associated with the process of victimisation, othering, and exclusion. Many activists complained that because of their pro-Euromaidan position, which was portrayed in propaganda outlets not as a fight for democracy but as the equivalent of a Ukrainian nationalistic position, inhabitants of the Donbas and Crimea were threatened and forced to leave the region. Thus, a differentiation was made, not along ethnic lines, but through political preferences.

In-depth interviews demonstrate that changes in official historical narrative and symbolic memoryscapes were among the main triggers provoking IDPs' reimagination of a sense of belonging to the local receiving communities as well as to the wider national or transnational communities such as the Ukrainian political nation, the Soviet Union, Eastern Slavic people, and the European space. In this process, history turned into an important interpretive resource for one's attachment or alienation. The imagined past may consist of selected symbolic markers, events, or historical figures that are seen as 'ours' and form a system that helps IDPs *to define their belonging*:

> I was born in 1964, I grew up in the Soviet Union. When they destroyed … when there was a division between Ukraine and Russia, it turned out that people were deprived of everything they believed in, and in return they received nothing (woman, old, resettled from Grolivka to Kharkiv, 2014).

This helps to explain current events – 'The situation is absolutely reminiscent of the revolution of 1917' – or to make a *nostalgic escape from their current reality.*

The analysis of IDPs' stories suggests that in the process of building their sense of belonging to the wider community (regional, national, or transnational), they relate to the same grand-narratives (the Ukrainian national, the Ukrainian Soviet, and the Russian imperial) and historical markers which constitute an important part in the memory 'wars' in Ukrainian society (as briefly described in the previous section). After Putin's denial of Ukraine's/ Ukrainian's existence allegedly based on 'historical facts', IDPs refer more often to the past as a part of reclaiming their denied identity and re-establishing their sense of belonging. The key historical period to which most respondents referred is the Soviet past (and especially the Second World War), although its usage and interpretations differ greatly.

Respondents from the Donbas report that in the past, the memories of older family members would often be limited to either nostalgic stories about the benefits of life in Soviet times (with an emphasis on their socio-professional achievements in the Soviet system) or glorification stories about their experience in the Second World War, structured according to the Soviet myth of the Great Patriotic War. As discussed earlier, this myth remains, in many cases, the central identity marker not only for residents of the Donbas and Crimea, but for the inhabitants of Ukraine. Accordingly, the attitude towards the Soviet glorification narrative of the 'Great Patriotic War' often becomes one of the key markers determining the boundaries of belonging. Respondents point to the tensions in their region created, in part, by government attempts to shift the celebration of Victory Day from May 9th, which continued the tradition of the Soviet celebrations of the glorious victory of the Red Army, to May 8th, representing this as Victory in Europe Day or The Day of Remembrance and changing it from a Ukrainian or post-Soviet memory space to a transnational one. In shifting the emphasis of the commemoration, the government sought to change its symbolic meaning from glorifying victory to the remembrance of victims. Simultaneously, it tried to link the Ukrainians' fight in the Second World War to the current fight, by calling the latter 'Ukraine's Great Patriotic

War'. The Ukrainian government's attempt to reassess the key elements and agents of the glorification narrative of the Great Patriotic War provoked the alienation of those citizens for whom the Soviet Ukrainian history narrative was still at the core of their sense of belonging, including the displaced population.

At the same time, as illustrated by Fedor, Lewis, and Zhurzhenko (2017), in the quasi-state entities 'D/LPR' and Russia, the tendencies were the opposite. The Great Patriotic War myth was fixed as a core identity marker and transformed from remembrance culture to re-enactment practices:

> They [the government of the quasi-state entities – author] immediately cut off Ukrainian channels, radio broadcasting, everything. They have Russian outlets all the time, with this Victory Day, for which they prepare all year round! They constantly have this theme! (Woman, middle-aged, resettled from Donetsk to Geneva, 2021)

An analysis of the public speeches by current Russian President Putin shows that the theme of the 'Great Patriotic war' and the 'denazification' of Ukrainians became absolutely central to the Kremlin's justifications for Russia's aggression against Ukraine. Timothy Snyder describes it as a war of aggression on European memory as it instrumentalises the key concepts of 'genocide' and 'Nazism'. Snyder argues that 'Putin is not just making them meaningless. He is debasing, perverting and taking them away. He creates a situation, where there is no connection between signifier and signified, no connection between rhetoric and reality' (Snyder, 2022). And later these concepts are used as labels of extreme othering. However, elements of this strategy have been tested in the temporarily occupied territories since 2014.

In their interviews, my interlocutors described how pro-Russian propaganda used historical controversies around the Second World War to set Ukrainians against each other and to increase divisions. For example, they cite numerous cases where propaganda outlets in Crimea and the Donbas altered the image of a controversial leader of the Ukrainian nationalist clandestine movement,[34] Bandera, by using the label ('*Banderite*') which then became a key marker of othering and pushing people with a pro-Ukrainian position out of the community. They describe cases when it was used even as the collective term for the

---

[34] Ukrainian Insurgent Army (UPA in Ukrainian) – 'The Second World War-era nationalist-led army, which has been a hot topic in Ukrainian politics since 2004. The UPA, whose soldiers are as much praised for their resistance to the communist regime as they are criticised or even vilified for participation in the ethnic cleansing of Poles, fought in the western regions of Galicia and Volhynia and has been part of the living memory of the local population. They saw the UPA condemned under the Soviet regime and celebrated during the years of independence' (Plokhii, 2017). On the formation of the Bandera image and commemorational practices see: Liebich & Myshlovska, 2014; Zaitsev, 2015; Yurchuk, 2017).

entire Ukrainian society (people living outside the temporarily occupied territories), calling them '*Banderites*'. The term 'Nazi' also was often used. This shows that othering and the denial of the right to belong can be caused not only by the demonstration of different ideological positions (pro-Ukrainian position – belonging by choice), but also by the simple fact of moving to the territory controlled by the government (belonging by exclusion). Propaganda built around selected historical markers aimed to form a sense of alienation in the inhabitants of the temporarily occupied territories from the rest of Ukrainian society (regardless of their ideological preferences). Some IDPs from the Donbas complained that they found themselves in a situation of double isolation – when residents of temporarily occupied territories call them 'Bandera traitors' and push them out of their home communities and then receiving communities, as some researchers show, treat them with suspicion that they are 'separatists'.

The use, in the popular discourse, of the Second World War myth as an important marker of belonging is not a unique feature of the Russian-Ukrainian conflict. Skey, in his study of belonging, entitlement, and the politics of immigration, shows that the Second World War myth functions as a marker that also defines boundaries of belonging and entitlement in British society (Skey, 2014, p. 5).

Interviews show that, similarly to the IDPs from the Donbas, Crimean Tatars' temporal sense of belonging is also built around the Soviet period, but at its core is an anti-Soviet victimisation narrative. A key marker around which everything is structured is the period of Stalin's deportation in 1944. Memories of this event form the basis of family stories. Having experienced prolonged persecution, Crimean Tatars developed the ability to preserve and transmit the history of their group through family narratives. My study shows that in a new forced relocation situation, Crimean Tatars successfully employ this strategy again. Their family stories are often structured as narratives that connect many historical events and periods not directly connected to family history, including the periods of the Crimean Khanate, the Ottoman and Russian Empires, and Soviet history. It is evident that the Crimean Tatar historical narrative structures their sense of belonging around the feeling of symbolic trauma (the 1944 deportation), where other reference points from the past (the seizure of Crimea by Catherine II) or present (the annexation of Crimea in March 2014) are incorporated. Such a structure also makes it more open to the inclusion of elements of a Ukrainian victimhood narrative (the Stalin-organised famine of 1933–34) and helps to 'inscribe' a Crimean Tatar narrative of belonging to the Ukrainian political nation. For this they use three strategies – a stress on common Soviet traumas, referring to symbolic markers, events, or historical figures of the

Ukrainian national pantheon, and an emphasis on common historical experiences.

Many interviewed IDPs from both regions reported that the recent crisis and relocation have prompted them or their family members to talk about issues that were previously silenced in their family narratives, including ethnic origins (Greek, Polish, etc.) and memories deemed 'problematic' by the Soviet system: Stalinist repression, dekulakisation, and the famine, for example. The 'forgotten' themes in family narratives often appear as a reaction to the recent developments in the Donbas and Crimea and have several functions. First, the 'invention' of a forgotten ethnic origin that helped them to claim assistance during the resettlement from the national-cultural organisations located in Ukraine and abroad. Second, previously silenced family stories appealing to common/similar experiences can be used as an argument for claiming belonging to their new communities. The resettlement of IDPs from both Crimea and the Donbas stimulated a process of (re)articulation of their sense of belonging. For this purpose, they actively utilise both personal (or family) memories, as well as their knowledge of the historical past. At the same time, their attitudes towards the past also change as a result of their encounters with new urban spaces and their symbolic markers. An understanding of all those mechanisms is important as the massive cross-border migration of Ukrainian displaced people has become a prominent international and national governance issue and a subject of political debate that exposes anxieties and concerns regarding the identities, hierarchies of belonging, and the historical memory in Ukraine and the wider region.

5 Conclusions

An examination of the main causes of the Russia-Ukrainian conflict before February 2022 and how it was seen in the scholarly literature demonstrates that many scholars in their interpretation of the nature of the conflict over the Donbas in 2014 often point to an identity war based on polarised identities and memory projects as the main factor in the conflict's escalation. Similar arguments were recently used by Putin in his justification of Russia's invasion of Ukraine. The data analysed in this Element show that this is a considerable misrepresentation and oversimplification. Firstly, opinion polls from 2015 consistently show that Ukrainians demonstrate growing support for the nation as a political entity. What is more, the outbreak of war and the displacement of large population groups can dramatically change the established landscape of social and national identities, hierarchies, and politics of belonging causing anxieties and concerns that lie at the heart of national identity and culture.

However, markers emphasising the importance of citizenship practices for Ukrainian identity appear to be highly important and relevant for respondents across Ukraine, and specifically in the Donbas region. Secondly, as it was shown, ethnic and linguistic lines do not coincide in Ukraine. Therefore, Ukrainians and Russians in Crimea and the Donbas cannot be described as two separate antagonistic national groups, but rather as strongly intertwined and mutually inclusive groups with blurred lines of group boundaries. This result has an important implication – it gives a very different perspective to the one presented by the Russian media and some international experts on the processes of identity building that were taking place in Crimea and in the Donbas region before 2014. Both regions had a strong sense of local/regional identity, but in terms of self-identification of nationality, the absolute majority of the inhabitants of the Donbas and Crimea saw themselves as a part of the Ukrainian political project.

My comparison of IDP experiences of resettlement in Ukraine reveals that:

- One cannot identify any specific division between ethnically Ukrainian or Russian IDPs.
- The only ethnocultural group that visibly stands out is the Crimean Tatar population.
- Those respondents who stayed in temporarily occupied territories demonstrated an absence of exclusivist Russian nationalistic narratives, a strong Donbas regional identity, and connectedness to the region. In national terms, a minority self-identified as Russians and the majority as Ukrainians. However, both groups used the Soviet formula of ascribed nationality and a harmonious coexistence of both ethnicities.

This study also shows that the role of the state in internal migration governance must be reconsidered. The analysed experiences of internally displaced populations from Crimea and the Donbas demonstrate that conflict-induced internal displacement creates legal situations and experiences comparable to cross-border migration – it is characterised by limited mobility and citizenship rights, integration challenges, and experiences of exclusion.

Current international guidance presupposes that the primary responsibility for offering humanitarian aid and fulfilling the IDPs' rights falls on their own states. Our study illustrates that pressures of a military conflict demand the state adopt new defence policies, which include the setting up of new de facto borders, establishing institutional, legal, and regulatory frameworks related to border-crossing and the confirmation of citizenship rights for those moving from the temporarily occupied territories. As a result, the IDPs are caught between the state's two missions: the mission of setting the new border order and its primary responsibility of offering them protection and humanitarian aid policies. The analysed data show that prior to 2022, the IDPs' exclusion in Ukraine was not so much based on ethnic or linguistic differences as on questioning or limiting their Ukrainian citizenship rights and freedoms ('uneven citizenship'). Moreover, state institutions and low-level bureaucracies are the main agents that repeatedly treated IDPs as alien, thus implicitly questioning their belonging to the community or national body.

The common practice for displaced people from Crimea and the Donbas, attempting to overcome state-imposed symbolic borders, was their active engagement in civil society networks. Social media and internet platforms are now important drivers for the IDPs' (as well as the receiving communities') self-organisation allowing for transborder, quick, and flexible responses to the changing needs of different groups and communities. Different ways of civic participation, both institutionalised and non-formal, gave the IDPs agency and enabled them to rebuild their lives, escaping unnecessary state categorisation and hierarchisation. IDPs became active agents of social change in the receiving communities through engagement in urban activism, 'rebranding', and gentrification of their new localities for touristic purposes, sharing information and resources and establishing missing people services. These activities not only empowered them, but also assisted their adaptation and helped them to negotiate their new place and to assert their identities and sense of belonging within the receiving communities. However, the IDPs came from different ethnic and cultural backgrounds, including the Muslim population of Crimea. As a result, their civil society engagement has differed formally and essentially by stressing different cultural markers of belonging.

The current debates around the pressing issues of immigration, when it comes to managing migration flows but also when it comes to its integration policies, are mostly concerned with the migrants' or refugees' access to economic resources, including jobs, health care, welfare benefits and housing, and political participation. Yet, analysis shows that they overlook the importance of historical memory and imagination. Temporal dimensions of belonging and symbolic markers present in the public space could become important factors that plays a role in processes of social inclusion and exclusion, stereotypisation and othering . They might provoke conflicts or create new lines of solidarity.

My research demonstrates that the dynamics of memory production can be influenced by seemingly invisible groups of 'refugees', both at the level of a locality and nationwide. Family memories and attitudes towards the past can be utilised by creating a sense of belonging to the community. The historical past could also become a part of new forms of social activism (many Ukrainian cities, in their search for new possibilities, started to reproduce European practices of the revitalisation of historical and industrial heritage sites by turning them into tourist attractions). Participation in such activities underscores the agency of the displaced. The Ukrainian case illustrates that IDP resettlement across the country created a novel dynamic in shaping a new sense of belonging and common memory.

As I was making the final proofs for this Element, Russia 'evacuated' a few thousand inhabitants of the temporarily occupied territory of the Donbas and placed them in refugee camps, built overnight, in the countryside, far from any cities, to create the picture of a 'humanitarian catastrophe' and a 'genocide' as an additional pretext for launching a full-scale war.

After the Russian attack, Ukraine's western neighbour Poland accepted close to 2 million Ukrainian refugees in the space of two weeks with the help of the civil society, without building a single refugee camp in the countryside. Ukraine, and especially its northern, eastern, and southern frontier regions are engulfed in the flames of war. These are the regions which already have the highest presence of IDPs. Now, once again, they have had to leave everything behind and flee, together with other Ukrainians. After less than a month of war, close to a third of Ukraine's population became displaced. At the same time, in defending their right to exist, Ukrainians draw massively on the experiences they learned during the Euromaidan and after: this includes civil society support and self-aid networking, a willingness to protest and show their commitment to freedom and the ability to defend democracy even in occupied cities. These practices of self-organisation and self-aid networking, described earlier, as well as various forms of activism aimed at supporting the displaced in Ukraine were quickly adopted to support those fleeing outside. Moreover, fleeing cross-border Ukrainians continued to demonstrate elevated levels of solidarity and self-organisation. They were reproducing learned patterns of self-organisation by creating social media self-aid networks and volunteer groups that provide various forms of assistance in their new receiving communities. Similar processes can be observed in Ukraine and its neighbouring countries – Germany, Poland, and others, where the response of civilian structures created by Ukrainians and locals has largely outpaced the more formal and cumbersome international aid organisations and state response. Our study shows that the whole logic of humanitarian aid for the displaced population of war-torn societies requires attention and rethinking. This situation shows the possibilities of self-organisation and self-aid networks, which have both an organised and spontaneous nature but at the same time manage to provide solutions to the problems of displaced Ukrainians. Future enquiries into the response of the population of the neighbouring countries to the arrival of millions of Ukrainians should focus more on these new forms of civic mobilisation and activism, which could provide a new model for international humanitarian aid campaigns.

However, like the post-2014 situation when the IDPs within Ukraine remained practically 'invisible' to migration research conducted in Europe, migration caused by the Russian mass-scale invasion is considered primarily as a cross-border phenomenon, while the phenomenon of IDPs, which is much bigger, remains almost overlooked: compare 6 million refugees with the Ukrainian government estimates of 4–10 million IDPs. After the most recent repeated Russian strikes on power plants and energy facilities across Ukraine, which left the majority of cities with blackouts and no running water or heat, this estimated number might grow significantly larger.

This new wave of displacement affects practically all regions of Ukraine and is also actively directed to the outside of the country. The visa-free regime, in combination with simplified procedures for admission, allowing war refugees from Ukraine to skip a lengthy asylum application process and giving temporary protection in the EU for up to three years, opened new possibilities for Ukrainian refugees. However, it created new lines of division because it is seen as a form of preferential treatment of Ukrainian refuges in the EU. At the same time, there is very little discussion around the nature of temporary protection which, by definition, is a fairly precarious status. In contrast to temporary protection status, refugee status is permanent, and thus is more secure. It also comes with rights that are incorporated into international law. Temporary protection is based on a political agreement and can be easily terminated. This war-induced migration in the wake of the Russian aggression poses pressing challenges not only to the Ukrainian receiving communities, but to many European countries. It is important to shape new lines of social inclusion and avoid exclusion through the production of multiple internal, physical, symbolic, and bureaucratic borders. The challenge for regional and global security now is combating the increasing weaponisation of refugees and the intentional creation of humanitarian crises as a war tactic, within the existing frameworks of global migration governance and conflict resolution.

Abbreviations

ATO – Anti-Terrorist Operation of Ukrainian government
CSOs – Civil society organisations
DCAF – Geneva Centre for Security Sector Governance
DPR (Donetsk People's Republic) – The quasi-state entity proclaimed as so-called 'people's republic' at the temporarily occupied part of Donetsk *oblast*
EECP – Exit-entry checkpoints
EU – European Union
GCA – Government-controlled areas
GDP – Gross domestic product
HURI – Ukrainian Research Institute at Harvard University
IBO – Identities-borders-orders model
IDP – Internally displaced people
LPR – (Luhansk People's Republic) – The quasi-state entity proclaimed as so-called 'people's republic' at the temporarily occupied part of Luhansk *oblast*
NATO – North Atlantic Treaty Organisation
NGO – Non-Governmental Organisation
OSCE – Organization for Security and Co-operation in Europe
R2P – Responsibility to Protect Principle
SCORE – Social Cohesion and Reconciliation
TOT – Temporarily occupied territories
UGCA – Ukraine's government-controlled areas
UNDP – United Nations Development Program
UNHCR – United Nations High Commissioner for Refugees
USAID – United States Agency for International Development
USSR – Union of Soviet Socialist Republics
WMR – World Migration Report
WWII – World War II/Second World War

Appendix 1

Two surveys form the basis for the analysis of regional specific Ukrainian citizens' involvement in different forms of civic engagement and self-aid activities as well as the cross-regional data analysis in the Element.

The first one is the survey 'State of charitable practices in Ukraine', carried out by the Socioinform Centre for the Zahoriy Foundation during the period July–August 2019 and July–August 2021 in all *oblasti* and parts of the Donbas controlled by the Ukrainian government, personal standardised face-to-face interviews were conducted, based on a multi-stage quota. The sample (*n* = 2,000 split proportionally between all *oblasti*) was aligned with age (respondents were aged eighteen and older) and gender quotas representative of Ukraine's profile with respect to the largest administrative units (*oblasti*), types of settlement (from villages to cities over 1 million), as recorded in official state statistics for 2019, with a margin of error of approximately 2.2 per cent.

The other includes two consecutive waves of the survey 'Region, Nation, and Beyond: An Interdisciplinary and Transcultural Reconsideration of Ukraine', carried out by the Socioinform Centre for the University of St Gallen project 'Region, Nation, and Beyond. An Interdisciplinary and Transcultural Reconceptualization of Ukraine' during the periods of March 2015 and 15 October–1 November 2017. In all *oblasti* and the parts of the Donbas controlled by the Ukrainian government, personal standardised face-to-face interviews were conducted, based on a multi-stage quota. The sample (*n* = 6,000 split proportionally between all *oblasti*) was aligned with age (respondents aged eighteen and older) and gender quotas representative of Ukraine's profile with respect to the largest administrative units (*oblasti*), types of settlement (from villages to cities over 1 million), as recorded in official state statistics for 2016, with a margin of error of approximately 2 per cent.

All opinion polls in Ukraine are currently not conducted for interviewers' and interviewees' safety in occupied Crimea or Donetsk and Luhansk parts. Population living on territories which are not under the control of the Ukrainian government as excluded from the sampling.

The quantitative data are used to uncover regional patterns in the level of engagement in civil society activities (financial donations, material goods donations, community service, etc.) in general and particularly in support of IDPs from Crimea and Donbas. As an independent variable I use a list representing the twenty-five biggest administrative units (twenty-four *oblasti* plus Kyiv City) of Ukraine, which later were also georeferenced for use in geospatial visualisation techniques. Regional variations in support of IDPs from Crimea and the Donbas were visualised using geospatial mapping techniques (the ArcMap programme), based on two variables 'support IDPs_2015' and 'support IDPs_2017' computed as the per cent of respondents who engaged in this activity for each *oblast* and Kyiv City.

Appendix 2

Question: 'In the last 12 months have you needed to ... (no more than 5 answers)'

1. Contact your local politician or manager
2. Sign a petition
3. Collect signatures yourself
4. Participate in a demonstration or rally
5. Participate in the boycott of certain goods or services
6. Provide assistance to internally displaced persons from Crimea and Eastern Ukraine
7. Provide assistance to the military in the anti-terrorist operation
8. To be engaged in volunteer activity
9. Invest your resources, tangible (donate things) or intangible (time, professional advice)
10. Participate in public fights
11. Address the media with a complaint or suggestions to solve problems
12. None of these actions
13. It is difficult to answer

Appendix 3

Table 1 Ethnic and language groups in Crimea and the Donbas, March 2013

Declared nationality, per cent			
Nationality	**Crimea (%)**	**Donetska** *oblast* **(%)**	**Luhanska** *oblast* **(%)**
Ukrainian	28	75	61
Russian	57	21	34
Other	14	4	2
Native language, per cent			
Language	**Crimea (%)**	**Donetska** *oblast* **(%)**	**Luhanska** *oblast* **(%)**
Ukrainian	8	11	4
Russian	66	47	54
Mixed (bilingual/ trilingual)	15	39	39
Other	11	3	1
Difficult to say	0	0	2
Language used at home, per cent			
Language	**Crimea (%)**	**Donetska** *oblast* **(%)**	**Luhanska** *oblast* **(%)**
Ukrainian	3	3	2
Russian	68	72	67
Mixed (bilingual/ trilingual)	9	22	16
Other	5	1	1
Difficult to say	15	3	14

Calculated by author.

Source: 'Region, Nation, and Beyond: An Interdisciplinary and Transcultural Reconsideration of Ukraine' survey, www.uaregio.org/en/surveys/methodology/.

Table 2 Importance of listed identities for the inhabitants of Donbas, Crimea, and other six neighbouring *oblasts* of Ukraine (a mean value for each listed identity on 5-point scale), March 2013

Oblasts	Locality	Region	Ukrainian	Russian	East Slavic	European	Professional	Generation	Religious community	Class
				(A mean value for each listed identity on a 5-point scale)						
Crimea	4.47	4.53	3.71	3.76	3.14	2.95	4.04	4.54	3.24	3.67
Khersonska	4.36	4.51	4.23	2.13	2.47	2.25	2.72	4.08	2.91	3.38
Mykolaivska	4.32	4.40	4.40	2.24	2.78	2.68	3.47	4.51	3.18	3.72
Odeska	4.41	4.51	3.92	2.83	3.15	2.71	3.79	4.43	3.62	3.96
Donetska	4.26	4.34	3.95	2.88	3.16	2.70	3.64	4.35	3.41	3.82
Luhanska	4.19	4.30	3.65	3.31	3.13	2.10	3.63	3.99	2.98	3.58
Kharkivska	4.41	4.42	4.22	2.58	2.83	2.98	3.68	4.48	3.18	4.01
Zaporizka	4.41	4.47	4.17	2.52	3.21	2.57	3.81	4.47	3.07	3.95
Dnipropetrovska	4.21	4.24	4.28	2.36	2.35	2.43	3.64	4.17	3.21	3.76
Ukraine	4.39	4.43	4.32	2.12	2.74	2.74	3.70	4.30	3.45	3.84

Calculated by author.

Source: 'Region, Nation, and Beyond: An Interdisciplinary and Transcultural Reconsideration of Ukraine' survey, www.uaregio.org/en/surveys/methodology/.

Table 3 Importance of listed identities for the inhabitants of Donbas and Crimea, who self-identified as Russians or Ukrainians, March 2013

Self-identify as Ukrainians
(a mean value for each listed identity on 5-point scale)

Oblasts	Locality	Region	Ukrainian	Russian	East Slavic	European	Professional	Generation	Religious community	Class
Crimea	4.46	4.51	4.39	3.11	3.00	2.65	4.01	4.55	3.89	3.93
Donetska	4.31	4.39	4.36	2.56	3.14	2.71	3.65	4.38	3.44	3.81
Luhanska	4.20	4.35	4.01	2.95	3.14	2.10	3.58	4.05	2.95	3.53

Self-identify as Russians
(a mean value for each listed identity on 5-point scale)

Oblasts	Locality	Region	Ukrainian	Russian	East Slavic	European	Professional	Generation	Religious community	Class
Crimea	4.47	4.52	3.42	4.35	3.15	2.98	4.00	4.53	2.87	3.51
Donetska	4.13	4.21	2.88	4.23	3.27	2.68	3.61	4.32	3.41	3.86
Luhanska	4.26	4.28	3.05	4.00	3.09	2.06	3.66	3.84	2.99	3.66

Calculated by author.

Source: 'Region, Nation, and Beyond: An Interdisciplinary and Transcultural Reconsideration of Ukraine' survey, www.uaregio.org/en/surveys/methodology/.

References

Aasland, A., Lyska, O. (2016). Local democracy in Ukrainian cities: Civic participation and responsiveness of local authorities. *Post-Soviet Affairs, 32* (2), 152–75. https://doi.org/10.1080/1060586X.2015.1037072.

Amoore, L., Marmura, S., Salter, M. B. (2008). Editorial: Smart borders and mobilities: Spaces, zones, enclosures. *Surveillance & Society, 5*(2), 96–101.

Barrington, L. W., Herron, E. (2004). One Ukraine or many? Regionalism in Ukraine and its political consequences. *Nationalities Papers, 32*(1), 53–86. https://doi.org/10.1080/0090599042000186179.

Beissinger, M. R. (2017). 'Conventional' and 'virtual' civil societies in autocratic regimes. *Comparative Politics, 49*(3), 351–71. https://doi.org/10.5129/ 001041517820934267.

Bekirova, H., Ivanets′ A., Tyshchenko. Yu., Hromenko, S., Ablayev, B. (2020). *Istoriya Krymu ta kryms′kotatars′koho narodu.* Kyiv: Kryms′ka rodyna.

Brubaker, R. (2001). The return of assimilation? Changing perspectives on immigration and its sequels in France, Germany, and the United States. *Ethnic and Racial Studies, 24*(4), 531–48. https://doi.org/10.1080/01419870120049770.

Bulakh, T. (2020). Entangled in social safety nets: Administrative responses to and lived experiences of internally displaced persons in Ukraine. *Europe-Asia Studies, 72*(3), 455–80. https://doi.org/10.1080/09668136 .2019.1687648.

Burlyuk, O., Shapovalova, N., Zarembo K. (Eds.). (2017). *Civil society in Ukraine: Building on Euromaidan legacy.* Kyiv: Kyiv Mohyla Law and Politics Journal. https://doi.org/10.18523/kmlpj119977.2017-3.1-22.

Charron, A. (2016). Whose is Crimea? Contested sovereignty and regional identity. *Region: Regional Studies of Russia, Eastern Europe, and Central Asia, 5*(2), 225–56. https://doi.org/10.1353/reg.2016.0017.

Cooley, A., Ron, J. (2002). The NGO scramble: Organizational insecurity and the political economy of transnational action. *International Security, 27*(1), 5–39. https://doi.org/10.1162/016228802320231217.

De Cordier, B. (2017). Ukraine's vendée war? A look at the 'resistance identity' of the Donbass insurgency. *Russian Analytical Digest, 198,* 2–6. https://doi .org/10.31205/ua.175.01.

DECAF Report (2021). Lukichov, V., Nikitiuk, T., Kravchenko, L. *Civil Society in Donbas, Ukraine: Organizations and Activities.* Switzerland: DCAF, Civil Society in Donbas, Ukraine: Organizations and Activities | DCAF – Geneva

Centre for Security Sector Governance, accessed 12 June 2021. www.dcaf.ch/sites/default/files/publications/documents/CivilSocietyDonbas.pdf.

Derzhavnyi Komitet Statystyky Ukrainy (2001). Pro Kilkist ta Sklad Naselennia Avtonomnoi Respubliky Krym za danymy Vseukrainskoho perepysu Nasellennia 2001 roku, http://2001.ukrcensus.gov.ua/results/general/nationality/crimea/, accessed 23 December 2021.

Earl, J., Kimport, K. (2011). *Digitally enabled social change: Activism in the Internet age.* Boston: Massachusetts Technological Institute Press. https://doi.org/10.7551/mitpress/9780262015103.001.0001.

FOA, R., Ekiert, G. (2017). The weakness of postcommunist civil society reassessed. *European Journal of Political Research, 56*(2), 419–39. https://doi-org.ezp-prod1.hul.harvard.edu/10.1111/1475-6765.12182.

European Commission (2022). *Migration management: Welcoming refugees from Ukraine.* https://home-affairs.ec.europa.eu/policies/migration-and-asylum/migration-management/migration-management-welcoming-refugees-ukraine_en, accessed 30 September 2022.

European Union Action Plan on Integration of the Third-Country Nationals (2016). Strasbourg, 7 June 2016. https://eur-lex.europa.eu/legal-content/EN/TXT/?uri=CELEX%3A52016DC0377&qid=1632298272980, accessed 2 September 2021.

Fedor, J. (2015). Russian media and the war in Ukraine. *Journal of Soviet and Post-Soviet Politics and Society, 1* (1), 1–6.

Fedor, J., Lewis, S., Zhurzhenko, T. (2017). *War and memory in Russia, Ukraine and Belarus.* Cham: Palgrave Macmillan. https://doi.org/10.1007/978-3-319-66523-8.

Filipchuk, L., Lomonosova, N., Slobodian, O. (2021). Study of the needs and challenges of civil society organizations that work with migrants and mobile populations. *CEDOS report.* https://cedos.org.ua/en/researches/potreby-ta-vyklyky-orhanizatsii-hromadianskoho-suspilstva-shcho-pratsiuiut-z-mihrant_kamy-ta-mobilnym-naselenniam/, accessed 11 May 2021.

Fisher, D. (2015). The Problem with research on activism. *Mobilizing Ideas,* 2 September. https://mobilizingideas.wordpress.com/2015/09/02/the-problem-with-research-on-activism/, accessed 13 June 2021.

Gatrell, P. (1999). *A whole empire walking: Refugees in Russia during World War I.* Bloomington: Indiana University Press, 141–70. https://doi.org/10.1086/ahr/105.5.1837

Gomza, I. (2019). Quenching fire with gasoline: Why flawed terminology will not help to resolve the Ukraine crisis. *PONARS Eurasia Policy Memo,* 576, www.ponarseurasia.org/node/10168, accessed 2 December 2021.

Grace, J., Mooney, E. D. (2009). Peacebuilding through the electoral participation of displaced populations. *Refugee Survey Quarterly, 28*(1), 95–121. https://doi.org/10.1093/rsq/hdp012.

GRID (2016). *Global report on internal displacement* (Geneva, Internal Displacement Monitoring Centre), www.internal-displacement.org/publica tions/ukraine-translating-idps-protection-intolegislative-action, accessed 3 July 2021.

Griffith, E. E. (1995). Personal storytelling and the metaphor of belonging. *Cultural Diversity and Mental Health, 1*(1), 29–37. https://doi.org/10 .1037/1099-9809.1.1.29.

Guibernau, M. (2013). *Belonging: Solidarity and division in modern societies.* Cambridge: Polity. https://doi.org/10.1017/s0047279414000452.

Hahn, G. M. (2018). *Ukraine over the edge: Russia, the West and the 'new Cold War'.* Jefferson: McFarland.

Haran, O., Yakovlyev, M., Zolkina, M. (2019). Identity, war, and peace: Public attitudes in the Ukraine-controlled Donbas. *Eurasian Geography and Economics, 60*(6), 684–708. https://doi.org/10.1080/15387216 .2019.1667845.

Howard, M. (2003). *The weakness of civil society in post-communist Europe.* Cambridge: Cambridge University Press. https://doi.org/10.1017/ cbo9780511840012.

Huntington, S. P. (1993). The clash of civilizations?: the debate Eds. Fouad Ajami, Robert L. Bartley, Liu Binyan, et al. New York, NY: Foreign Affairs.

InfoSapience (2022). *61% ukrayintsiv stavlyat'sya do vymushenykh pereselentsiv pozytyvno ta spivchutlyvo, ale 5% – nehatyvno*, 6 June. https://sapiens .com.ua/ua/publication-single-page?id=232, accessed 1 October 2022.

Isański, J., Marek, N., Michalski, M. A., Sereda, V., Vakhitova, H. (2022). *Social reception and inclusion of refugees from Ukraine.* UKREF Research Report 1. www.researchgate.net/publication/361049486_Social_Reception_and_ Inclusion_of_Refugees_From_Ukraine, accessed 20 September 2022, DOI: 10.13140/RG.2.2.28450.9184.

Johnson, C., Jones, R., Paasi, A. et al. (2011). Interventions on rethinking 'the border' in Border Studies. *Political Geography, 30*(2), 61–9. https://doi.org/ 10.1016/j.polgeo.2011.01.002.

KIIS (2022). *Indicators of national-civic Ukrainian identity*, 16 August. www .kiis.com.ua/?lang=eng&cat=reports&id=1131&page=3, accessed 30 September 2022.

Koser, K. (2011). *Responding to migration from complex humanitarian emergencies: Lessons learned from Libya.* London: Chatham House.

Koval, N., Kulyk, V., Riabchuk, M., Zarembo, K., Fakhurdinova, M. (2022). Morphological analysis of narratives of the Russian-Ukrainian conflict in western academia and think-tank community. *Problems of Post-Communism*, *69*(2), 166–78. https://doi.org/10.1080/10758216.2021.2009348.

Krasniqi, G., Stjepanović, D. (2015). Uneven citizenship: Minorities and migrants in the post-Yugoslav space. *Ethnopolitics*, *14*(2), 113–20. https://doi .org/10.1080/17449057.2014.991153.

Krasynska, S., Eric, M. (2017). The formality of informal civil society: Ukraine's Euromaidan. *Voluntas*, *28*, 420–49. https://doi.org/10.1007/s11266-016-9819-8.

Kulyk, V. (2016). National identity in Ukraine: Impact of Euromaidan and the war. *Europe-Asia Studies*, *68*(4), 588–608. https://doi.org/10.1080/09668136 .2016.1174980.

Kuromiya, H. (1998). *Freedom and terror in the Donbas : a Ukrainian-Russian borderland, 1870s–1990s*. New York : Cambridge University Press.

Kuromiya, H. (2003). *Freedom and terror in the Donbas: A Ukrainian-Russian borderland, 1870s–1990s*. Cambridge: Cambridge University Press. https:// doi.org/10.1086/ahr/104.4.1420.

Kuzio, T. (2015). Competing nationalisms, Euromaidan, and the Russian-Ukrainian conflict. *Studies in Ethnicity and Nationalism*, 15(1), 157–69. https://doi.org/10.1111/sena.12137.

Kuznetsova, I., Mikheieva, O. (2020). Forced displacement from Ukraine's war-torn territories: Intersectionality and power geometry. *Nationalities Papers*, *48*(4), 690–706. https://doi.org/10.1017/nps.2020.34.

Kymlicka, W. (2010). The rise and fall of multiculturalism? New debates on inclusion and accommodation in diverse societies. *International Social Science Journal*, *61*(199), 97–112. https://doi.org/10.1111/j.1468-2451 .2010.01750.x.

Lazarenko, V. (2021). Renaming and reclaiming urban spaces in Ukraine: The perspective of internally displaced people. *Nationalities Papers*, *50*(3), 430–49. https://doi.org/10.1017/nps.2021.26.

Lewicka, M. (2007). Regional differentiation of identity: A comparison of Poland and Ukraine. *Studia Regionalne i Lokalne*, *8*, 21–51.

Lewicka, M. (2013) Place inherited or place discovered? Agency and communion in people-place bonding. *Studies in Psychology*, *34*(3), 261–74. https:// doi.org/10.1174/021093913808295154.

Lewicka, M., Iwańczak, B. (2019). The regional differentiation of identities in Ukraine: How many regions? In *Regionalism without Regions: Reconceptualizing Ukraine's Heterogeneity*. Eds. Schmid, U., Myshlovska, O. Budapest: Central European University Press, pp. 25–66.

Liebich, A., Myshlovska, O. (2014). Bandera: Memorialization and commemoration. *Nationalities Papers*, *42*(5), 750–70. https://doi.org/10.1080/00905992.2014.916666.

Liebich, A., Myshlovska, O., Sereda, V. (2019). The Ukrainian past and present: Legacies, memory and attitudes. In *Regionalism without Regions: Reconceptualizing Ukraine's Heterogeneity*. Eds. Myshlovska O., Schmid, U. Budapest: Central European University Press, pp. 67–134.

Lipsky, M. (1980). *Street-level bureaucracy: Dilemmas of the individual in public services*. New York: Russell Sage Foundation. https://doi.org/10.1177/003232928001000113.

Lubbers, M. J., Molina, J. L., McCarty, C. (2007). Personal networks and ethnic identifications: The case of migrants in Spain. *International Sociology*, *22*(6), 721–41. https://doi.org/10.1177/0268580907082255.

Lutsevych, O. (2013). *How to finish a revolution: Civil society and democracy in Georgia, Moldova and Ukraine*. London: Chatham House.

Lutz, P. (2017). Two logics of policy intervention in immigrant integration: An institutionalist framework based on capabilities and aspirations. *Comparative Migration Studies*, *5*(19), 1–18. https://doi.org/10.1186/s40878-017-0064-0.

Maliarchuk, N. (2011). *Rosiany v Donbasi (20-30 rr. XX st.)*. Donetsk: Chernetska.

Malyarenko, T., Wolff, S. (2018). The logic of competitive influence-seeking: Russia, Ukraine, and the conflict in Donbas. *Post-Soviet Affairs*, *34*(4), 191–212. https://doi.org/10.1080/1060586x.2018.1425083.

Malynovska, O. (2020). International migration of the Ukrainian population since independence. *Migration from the Newly Independent States*, *25*, 169–85. https://doi.org/10.1007/978-3-030-36075-7_8.

Matveeva, A. (2016). No Moscow stooges: Identity polarization and guerrilla movements in Donbass. *Southeast European and Black Sea Studies*, 16(1), 25–50. https://doi.org/10.1080/14683857.2016.1148415.

May, V. (2011). Self, belonging and social change. *Sociology*, *45*(3), 363–78. https://doi.org/10.1177/0038038511399624.

May, V. (2013). *Connecting self to society: Belonging in a changing world*. Macmillan International Higher Education. Basingstoke, Hampshire: Palgrave Macmillan. https://doi.org/10.1007/978-1-137-36726-6_10.

Mearsheimer, J. J. (2014). Why the Ukraine crisis is the west's fault: The liberal delusions that provoked Putin? *Foreign Affairs*, *93*, 77–89.

Mendelson, S. E., Glenn, J. K. (Eds.). (2002). *The power and limits of NGOs: A critical look at building democracy in Eastern Europe and Eurasia*. New York : Columbia University Press.

Menjívar, C., Abrego, L. (2012). Legal violence: Immigration law and the lives of Central American immigrants. *American Journal of Sociology*, *117*(5), 1380–421. https://doi.org/10.1086/663575.

Mikheieva, O., Sereda, V. (2015). Suchasni ukrainski vnutrishno peremishcheni osoby: Osnovni prychyny, stratehii pereselennia ta problemy adaptatsii. *Stratehii transformatsii i preventsii prykordonnykh konfliktiv v Ukraini. Zbirka analitychnykh materialiv 2014–2015.* Lviv: Halytska vydavnycha spilka, 9–49.

Ministersvtvo Sotsialnoi Polityky Ukrainy (2021). *Vnutrishnio Peremishcheni Osoby.* 6 July 2021, www.msp.gov.ua/timeline/Vnutrishno-peremishcheni-osobi.html, accessed 15 November 2021.

Mooney, E. D. (2001). Principles of protection for internally displaced persons. *International Migration*, *38*(6), 81–101. https://doi.org/10.1111/1468-2435 .00144.

Mudde, P. (2018). *Perspectives on the role of local initiatives to help IDPs: A qualitative research on the contribution of civil society organizations in Ukraine to the improvement of the socio-economic situation of IDPs.* Nijmegen: Radboud University.

Mykhnenko, V. (2011). *The political economy of post-communism: The Donbas and Upper Silesia in transition.* Saarbrücken: Lambert Academic.

Mykhnenko, V. (2020). Causes and consequences of the war in Eastern Ukraine: An economic geography perspective. *Europe-Asia Studies*, *72*(3), 528–60. https://doi.org/10.1080/09668136.2019.1684447.

Osipian, A. (2015). Historical myths, enemy images, and regional identity in the Donbass insurgency (Spring 2014). *Journal of Soviet and Post-Soviet Politics and Society*, *1*(1), 109–40. https://doi.org/10.3200/demo.14.4.495 -517.

Paasi, A. (2011). Borders, theory and the challenge of relational thinking. *Political Geography*, *30*(2), 62–3. https://doi.org/10.1016/b978-0-08-102295-5.10487-1.

Paasi, A. (2012). Border studies reanimated: Going beyond the territorial/ relational divide. *Environment and Planning*, *44*(10), 2303–09. https://doi .org/10.1068/a45282.

van der Pijl, K. (2018). *Flight MH17, Ukraine and the new Cold War.* Manchester: Manchester University Press. https://doi.org/10.7765/ 9781526131089.00007.

Plokhii, S. (2017). *Goodbye Lenin: A memory shift in revolutionary Ukraine*, http://gis.huri.harvard.edu/contemporary-atlas/revolution-of-dignity/lenin fall.html, accessed 11 October 2019.

Popescu, N. (2013). The Russia-Ukraine trade spat. *European Union Institute for Security Studies*, *26*, 1–2.

Portnov, A. (2015). Post-Maidan Europe and the new Ukrainian studies. *Slavic Review*, *74*(4), 723–31. https://doi.org/10.5612/slavicreview.74.4.723.

Probyn, E. (1996). *Outside belongings*. New York: Routledge. https://doi.org/10.4324/9781315865805.

de Ploeg, C. K. (2017). *Ukraine in the crossfire*. Atlanta: Clarity Press.

Rating (2022). *Seventeenth national survey: Identity. Patriotism. Values*, 17–18 August. https://ratinggroup.ua/en/research/ukraine/s_mnadcyate_zagalnonac_onalne_opituvannya_dentichn_st_patr_otizm_c_nnost_17-18_serpnya_2022.html, accessed 23 September 2022.

Region, Nation, and Beyond: An Interdisciplinary and Transcultural Reconsideration of Ukraine survey (2013, 2015, 2017). www.uaregio.org/en/surveys/methodology/, accessed 1 September 2021.

Ryabchuk, M. (2003). *Dvi Ukrainy: Realni mezhi virtualni vijni*. Kiev: Kritika.

Sakwa, R. (2014). *Frontline Ukraine: Crisis in the borderlands*. London: Bloomsbury. https://doi.org/10.5040/9780755603756.

Sardelić, J. (2015). Romani minorities and uneven citizenship access in the post-Yugoslav space. *Ethnopolitics*, *14*(2), 159–79. https://doi.org/10.1080/17449057.2014.991154.

Sasse, G. (2007). *The Crimea question: Identity, transition, and conflict*. Cambridge, MA: Harvard University Press.

Sasse, G. (2010). Ukraine: The role of regionalism. *Journal of Democracy*, *21*(3), 99–106. https://doi.org/10.1353/jod.0.0177.

Sasse, G., Lackner, A. (2018). War and identity: The case of the Donbas in Ukraine. *Post-Soviet Affairs*, 34(2–3), 139–57.

SCORE (2022). *Social cohesion in Ukraine part II: Towards a tolerant, cohesive and inclusive society*, June 2022. https://api.scoreforpeace.org/storage/pdfs/REP_DGEUkr21_SocCoh_II_v17.pdf, accessed 23 September 2022.

Schmid, U., Myshlovska, O. (Eds.). (2019). *Regionalism without regions: Reconceptualizing Ukraine's heterogeneity*. Budapest: Central European University Press.

Sereda, V. (2002). Regional historical identities in Ukraine: Case study of Lviv and Donetsk. *Naukovi Zapysky Natsionalnogo Universytetu Kyevo-Mohylanska Akademia*, *20*, 26–34.

Sereda, V. (2016). "Transformation of Identities and Historical Memories in Ukraine after the Euromaidan: National, Regional, Local Dimensions" Paper presented at the Annual Danyliw Research Seminar on Contemporary Ukraine, Chair of Ukrainian Studies. University of Ottawa. 10–12 November http://bit.ly/2uwEQwB.

Sereda, V. (2006). Rehionalni vymiry ukrainskoho sotsiumu: istorychne mynule i natsionalni identychnosti. *Agora, 3*, 29–41.

Sereda, V. (2020). 'Social distancing' and hierarchies of belonging: The case of displaced population from Donbas and Crimea. *Europe-Asia Studies, 72*(3), 404–31. https://doi.org/10.1080/09668136.2020.1719043.

Siriwardhana, C., Stewart, R. (2013). Forced migration and mental health: Prolonged internal displacement, return migration and resilience. *International Health, 5*(1), 19–23. https://doi.org/10.1093/inthealth/ihs014.

Skey, M. (2011). *National belonging and everyday life: The significance of nationhood in an uncertain world.* London: Palgrave.

Skey, M. (2014). 'How do you think I feel? It's my country': Belonging, entitlement and the politics of immigration. *The Political Quarterly, 85*(3), 326–32. https://doi.org/10.1111/1467-923x.12094.

Smal, V. (2016). *A great migration: What is the fate of Ukraine's internally displaced persons.* VoxUkraine, 30 June. https://voxukraine.org/en/great-migration-how-many-internally-displaced-personsare-there-in-ukraine-and-what-has-happened-to-them-en/, accessed 9 November 2019.

Soliman, K., Sereda, V., Fischer, J., Havrysh, O. (2022). *Aus der Ukraine nach Thüringengeflohen – Ergebnisse einer landesweiten Befragung.* Erfurt: IKPE.

Stewart, S., Dollbaum, J. M. (2017). Civil society development in Russia and Ukraine: Diverging paths. *Communist and Post-Communist Studies, 50*(3), 207–20. https://doi.org/10.1016/j.postcomstud.2017.08.001.

Tronc, E., Nahikian, A. (2020). *Ukraine conflict in the Donbas: Civilians hostage to adversarial geopolitics.* Cambridge: Harvard Humanitarian Initiative. https://doi.org/10.2139/ssrn.3657394.

UNDP (2016). *Building inclusive societies and sustaining peace through democratic governance and conflict prevention: An integrated approach.* New York: United Nations Development Programme, www.undp.org/sites/ g/files/zskgke326/files/publications/UNDP-GOVERNANCE%20AND% 20PEACEBUILDING_final.pdf, accessed 21 July 2021.

USAID (2017). Dixit, A., Einhorn, J., Fedin, J., Han, S., Li, M., Plekenpol, R., Zhang, K. *Analysis of Civil Society in Ukraine.* PRS Policy Brief 1617-01. 23 January 2017. Hanover: Nelson A. Rockefeller Centre for Public Policy and the Social Sciences, Dartmouth College. https://rockefeller .dartmouth.edu/report/analysis-civil-society-ukraine.

UNHCR (2016). *Ukraine UNHCR operational update 14 May–10 June 2016.* https://reliefweb.int/sites/reliefweb.int/files/resources/UNHCR% 20Operational%20Update%20on%20the%20Ukraine%20Situation%20-% 2014MAY-10JUN16.pdf, accessed 11 July 2021.

UNCHR (2021). *Refugees and asylum-seekers from Ukraine.* https://unhcr-web.github.io/refugee-statistics/0001-Vis-PoCs/Ukrainians.html, accessed 21 December 2021.

UNHCR (2022). *Internally Displaced Persons (IDP).* www.unhcr.org/ua/en/internally-displaced-persons, accessed 01 October 2022.

Vasquez, J. A. (2009). *The war puzzle revisited.* Cambridge: Cambridge University Press.

Vertovec, S. (2011). The cultural politics of nation and migration. *Annual Review of Anthropology, 40,* 241–56. https://doi.org/10.1146/annurev-anthro-081309-145837.

Way, L. (2014). The Maidan and Beyond: Civil Society and Democratization. *Journal of Democracy 25*(3), 35–43. doi: 10.1353/jod.2014.0042.

Wilson, A. (1995). The Donbas between Ukraine and Russia: The use of history in political disputes. *Journal of Contemporary History, 30*(2), 265–89.

Wilson, A. (2015). *The Ukrainians: Unexpected nation.* New Heaven: Yale University Press. https://doi.org/10.1086/ahr/107.5.1667.

Wilson, A. (2016). The Donbas in 2014: Explaining civil conflict perhaps, but not civil war. *Europe-Asia Studies, 68*(4), 631–52. https://doi.org/10.1080/09668136.2016.1176994.

Worschech, S. (2017). New civic activism in Ukraine: Building society from scratch? *Kyiv-Mohyla Law and Politics Journal, 3,* 23–45. https://doi.org/10.18523/kmlpj119984.2017-3.23-45.

World Migration Report (2020). *International Organization for Migration.* https://publications.iom.int/system/files/pdf/wmr_2020.pdf, accessed 15 July 2021.

Yekelchyk, S. (2015). *The conflict in Ukraine: What everyone needs to know?* New York: Oxford University Press.

Yekelchyk, S. (2016). *Stalin's empire of memory.* Toronto: University of Toronto Press.

Yukich, G. (2015). *Who gets left out when we talk about 'activism'?* Mobilizing Ideas, 2 September, https://mobilizingideas.wordpress.com/2015/09/02/the-problem-with-research-on-activism/, accessed 15 May 2021.

Yurchuk, Y. (2017). Reclaiming the past, confronting the past: OUN–UPA memory politics and nation building in Ukraine (1991–2016). In *War and Memory in Russia, Ukraine and Belarus.* Cham: Palgrave Macmillan, pp. 107–37. https://doi.org/10.1007/978-3-319-66523-8_4.

Yuval-Davis, N. (2006). Belonging and the politics of belonging. *Patterns of Prejudice, 40*(3), 197–214. https://doi.org/10.1080/00313220600769331.

Yuval-Davis, N. (2011). *The politics of belonging: Intersectional contestations.* London: Sage.

Zaitsev, O. (2015). De-mythologizing Bandera: Towards a scholarly history of the Ukrainian nationalist movement. *Journal of Soviet and Post-Soviet Politics and Society, 1*(2), 411–20.

Zayarnyuk, A. (2022). Historians as enablers? Historiography, imperialism, and the legitimization of Russian aggression. *East/West: Journal of Ukrainian Studies, 9*(2), 186–206.

Zayarnyuk, A., & Sereda, O. (2022). The Intellectual Foundations of Modern Ukraine: The Nineteenth Century. London: Routledge.https://doi.org/10.4324/9780429445705

Zhukov, Y. (2016). Trading hard hats for combat helmets: The economics of rebellion in eastern Ukraine. *Journal of Comparative Economics, 44*(1), 1–15. https://doi.org/10.1016/j.jce.2015.10.010.

Acknowledgements

My work on this project was supported by a semester-long URIS research fellowship at the University of Basel and a ten-month research fellowship at the Imre Kertész Kolleg in Jena. The maps used in this Element resulted from my research stay at the Ukrainian Research Institute at Harvard University where I worked on a digital atlas of social changes in Ukrainian society. An important part of research data was collected within the project 'Region, Nation and Beyond: An Interdisciplinary and Transcultural Reconceptualization of Ukraine' organised by the University of St Gallen in Switzerland. Lubomyr Hajda, Sarah King, and colleagues from the Post-Communist Politics and Economics Workshop of the Davis Centre for Russian and Eurasian Studies at Harvard University read parts of my text providing valuable comments and suggestions. At different stages, Olena Jennings, Sean Gaston, Jaime Elizabeth Hyatt, and Catherine Alexander skilfully edited my awkward English.

Cambridge Elements ☰

Global Development Studies

Peter Ho
Zhejiang University

Peter Ho is Distinguished Professor at Zhejiang University and high-level National Expert of China. He has held or holds the position of, amongst others, Research Professor at the London School of Economics and Political Science and the School of Oriental and African Studies, Full Professor at Leiden University and Director of the Modern East Asia Research Centre, Full Professor at Groningen University and Director of the Centre for Development Studies. Ho is well-cited and published in leading journals of development, planning and area studies. He published numerous books, including with *Cambridge University Press*, *Oxford University Press*, and *Wiley-Blackwell*. Ho achieved the William Kapp Prize, China Rural Development Award, and European Research Council Consolidator Grant. He chairs the International Conference on Agriculture and Rural Development (www.icardc.org) and sits on the boards of Land Use Policy, Conservation and Society, China Rural Economics, Journal of Peasant Studies, and other journals.

Servaas Storm
Delft University of Technology

Servaas Storm is a Dutch economist who has published widely on issues of macroeconomics, development, income distribution & economic growth, finance, and climate change. He is a Senior Lecturer at Delft University of Technology. He obtained a PhD in Economics (in 1992) from Erasmus University Rotterdam and worked as consultant for the ILO and UNCTAD. His latest book, co-authored with C.W.M. Naastepad, is *Macroeconomics Beyond the NAIRU* (Harvard University Press, 2012) and was awarded with the 2013 Myrdal Prize of the European Association for Evolutionary Political Economy. Servaas Storm is one of the editors of *Development and Change* (2006–now) and a member of the Institute for New Economic Thinking's Working Group on the Political Economy of Distribution.

Advisory Board
Arun Agrawal, *University of Michigan*
Jun Borras, *International Institute of Social Studies*
Daniel Bromley, *University of Wisconsin-Madison*
Jane Carruthers, *University of South Africa*
You-tien Hsing, *University of California, Berkeley*
Tamara Jacka, *Australian National University*

About the Series
The Cambridge Elements on Global Development Studies publishes ground-breaking, novel works that move beyond existing theories and methodologies of development in order to consider social change in real times and real spaces.

Cambridge Elements ☰

Global Development Studies

Printed in the United States
by Baker & Taylor Publisher Services